NATASHA

Vygotskian Dialogues

D0143817

NATASHA

Vygotskian Dialogues

Matthew Lipman

Teachers College, Columbia University
New York and London

Published by Teachers College Press, 1234 Amsterdam Avenue, New York, NY 10027

The introduction to this volume, "Squaring Russian Theory with American Practice," originally appeared in the May 1991 issue of *Educational Leadership* under the title "Squaring Soviet Theory with American Practice." Reprinted by permission of the American Society for Curriculum Development.

The outline "Forming a Philosophical Community of Inquiry" is reprinted from *Thinking in Education* by Matthew Lipman. Copyright © 1991 by Cambridge University Press. Reprinted with the permission of Cambridge University Press.

Library of Congress Cataloging-in-Publication Data

Lipman, Matthew.
    Natasha : Vygotskian dialogues / Matthew Lipman.
        p.   cm.
    Includes bibliographical references and index.
    ISBN 0-8077-3517-5. — ISBN 0-8077-3516-7 (pbk. : alk. paper)
    1. Vygotskiĭ, L. S. (Lev Semenovich), 1896–1934.
    2. Psychologists—Soviet Union.   3. Learning, Psychology of.
    4. Educational psychology.   I. Title.
    BF109.V95L56   1996
    150'.92—dc20   95-52526

ISBN 0-8077-3516-7 (paper)
ISBN 0-8077-3517-5 (cloth)

Printed on acid-free paper
Manufactured in the United States of America

03 02 01 00 99 98 97 96   8 7 6 5 4 3 2 1

CONTENTS

PREFACE

Natasha was written in December of 1991, and, as far as I was concerned, quite unexpectedly. Partly, I suppose, I wanted to clarify my own understanding of Davydov's educational psychology and its connection with Vygotsky, whom Stephen Toulmin has appropriately called the Mozart of psychology. Partly, I wanted to see if I could demonstrate some of Vygotsky's principles in the form of a fictional thought-experiment — for example, that thinking is the internalization of speech, and that reciprocal behavior plays an important role in learning to think. But almost from the start, a different agenda superseded, and this had to do with the role of the interview of an inquirer as an inquiry into inquiry. Natasha, the Ukrainian reporter whom I invented and who is presented as having been sent from China to interview me, flattered me by taking my inquiry seriously and by taking equally seriously her own study of what I was doing. But her primary interest, she indicated, was less in the substance of my inquiry than in its method. This, it seemed to me, might be a neat way of separating out the substantive aspects of an analysis from its procedural aspects, and I was game to pursue it as far as I could.

As to the interweaving of fact and fiction, I think it hardly necessary to apologize for what is, nowadays, not an unusual way of writing. Natasha, her family, and her friends are totally fictional characters; however, I am not, as far as the conventional understanding of the word "fictional" is concerned. Obviously, my own conversations with a fictional being must be considered fictional, too, to say nothing of my own fanciful representations of myself.

Needless to say, the kind of cognitive play I engage in, in Natasha, enormously increases the already marginal status of the work and, thereby, reduces its potential value as an *introductory* reading. Students awash in secondary texts and half-drowning in interpretations that pretend to be impartial and objective are not likely to welcome a study in which truth and make-believe masquerade as one another, in which the characters themselves discover that nothing is what it is assumed to be, and in which the very purpose of the book is an enigma. Yet I would maintain that these considerations do not disqualify *Natasha* from being a surrogate for philosophy itself, which has always sought to provide a hospitable dwelling for both rationality and imagination, which endlessly searches for the masks that underlie each successive unmasking, and which is as perplexed about its own identity as it is about anything else in the world.

The development of the Philosophy for Children curriculum was, through and through, purposeful. The development of *Natasha* was, in contrast — to adopt Kant's phrase — purposely purposeless. The less I understood why I was writing it, the more disinterestedly I devoted myself to it. I suspect the impetus was neither pedagogical, nor philosophical, nor psychological, but a bizarre gallimaufry that defied classification. Perhaps what it begins to resemble is Diderot's *Le Neveu de Rameau*, a story that Diderot could not bring himself to publish and that, likewise, consists of a conversation between the author and one other person. Or perhaps it tries to do for philosophy what Escher does for painting, presenting such paradoxes as ducks turning into fish and fish into ducks right before our eyes.

This preface is succeeded by an introduction that was written shortly after my first visit to Russia. It details some of the events that led up to that visit and sketches some of the theoretical background that will help explain the philosophical and psychological setting for my visit.

Since most readers are unlikely to be familiar with the innovative curriculum known as Philosophy for Children, I have provided, as a kind of second introduction, a chronology of major events in the history of that curriculum. A few samples of the children's texts are provided in *Natasha* itself.

Following *Natasha*, I have provided an afterword by Dr. Arkady Margolis, Rector of the International College of Education (ICE) in Moscow and a leader of efforts by the Russian government to develop teacher-education procedures for Russian elementary school teachers. Dr. Margolis is in charge of dissemination of early elementary Philosophy for Children programs throughout Siberia. He has also had lengthy experience in working with Dr. V. V. Davydov, Vice President of the Russian Academy of Education, and with Dr. Vitaly Rubtsov, Director of the Institute of Psychology, Academy of Science, Moscow. No one is more knowledgeable as to how Philosophy for Children has fitted into Russia's plans to overhaul its educational system and put it on a new footing that will be more in keeping with the important theoretical understandings derived from Vygotsky and Luria. At the same time, these are the Russian psychologists who recognize the link between the *activity* theory of Vygotsky and Luria on the one hand, and the pragmatic approach of Dewey and Mead on the other. The fact that these leaders of present-day Russian education are actively and energetically exploring these connections is one of the most encouraging aspects of what is taking place on the world educational stage at the present moment.

INTRODUCTION

Squaring Russian Theory with American Practice

As I begin preparing this account, I am in a British Airways plane leaving Moscow. Now that my brief visit to Russia is over, I have a few moments to reflect on what was accomplished. Outstanding, without a doubt, was the co-signing of an agreement by Dr. V. V. Davydov, Vice President of Russia's top educational research organization, the Academy of Pedagogical Sciences, and myself, as Director of the Institute for the Advancement of Philosophy for Children at Montclair State College in New Jersey. What I would like to relate is how that agreement — unexpected by both parties — came about.

Since my narrative must have a beginning, I shall let its starting point be the 1920s, a decade of brilliant activity by the Soviet scholar Lev Vygotsky. Far from being a narrow specialist, Vygotsky was deeply immersed in problems of art and creativity, as well as in philosophy and other humanistic approaches to knowledge and understanding. Yet all the while his attention was focusing more and more on psychology — in particular, the psychology of thinking, which he saw as central to education. Here, his restless energy and wide-ranging compassion led him in the direction of the education of the blind, the deaf, and other disabled individuals, particularly children. The study of those with perceptual and learning deficiencies suggested to him that he should concentrate his efforts on the analysis of the dynamic concept of thinking rather than on the relatively inert and elusive notion of intelligence, even though his theory of "proximal intelligence" is of substantial importance.

To Vygotsky, with his penchant for a behavioral interpretation of mind, thinking had to be understood as internalized activity, the genesis of our thoughts being explainable in terms of the overt, external activities — particularly the linguistic activities — in which we had been, and continued to be, engaged. These activities Vygotsky understood to be primarily social. They, and the connections that hold among them, are re-presented or reanimated in the life of the mind by a process of internalization. Our thoughts and the relationships among them tend to correspond roughly to what we and others say and do in the world. Suppose, for example, that the stance of a teacher in an early elementary school classroom is one of overwhelming authority and it is only the teacher who generally displays originality, independence, and thoughtfulness. The students, consequently, may tend to be merely reactive and hesitate to show intellectual initiative. The only classroom behavior that stimulates them is the teacher's questioning, to which they provide the expected responses. If I find myself in such a classroom, I will likely identify with my peers and behave — and think — as they do, although there are, of course, exceptions. What can snap me out of this cognitive lethargy, Vygotsky is suggesting, is lively classroom discourse, in which my classmates and I set models for each other of animated, thoughtful, and rational individuals quite capable of thinking for ourselves rather than waiting always to react to questions from the teacher.

Vygotsky's account of the social origins of thinking clearly called for a reconstruction of the classroom so that vigorous and reasonable dialogue would form a matrix that would, in turn, generate the children's thinking — thinking that would be correspondingly vigorous and reasonable. The stilted thinking that characterizes so many children after they have been in school for a while is a direct consequence of the stultified and stultifying behavior of their classmates who have not been permitted to conduct themselves as a reflective community. In this one masterful stroke, Vygotsky laid bare what is probably the most common cause of miseducation — the failure to convert the classroom into a community of discursive inquiry — and pointed out the direction in which educators had to go if the situation were to be corrected. But Vygotsky did not live to implement his theories; by the early 1930s, at the age of 38, he was dead of tuberculosis.

I should remark, in passing, that Vygotsky's theory may throw a bit of light on a notorious historical enigma: how it happened that certain small towns of barely 30,000 inhabitants — I am thinking of Athens of the 6th and 5th centuries B.C. and of Florence of the 14th and 15th centuries A.D. — could have achieved such an intensity of artistic and scientific creativity. The explanation that brilliant people from all over the world gravitated to these spots may be correct as far as it goes, but it is weak. It is more helpful to recognize that these towns were *communities of inquiry* in which discovery and invention everywhere stimulated fresh thinking, which, in turn, stimulated new discoveries and new inventions. Societies that do not aspire to be communities of inquiry may have to resign themselves to the fact that neither freedom nor justice nor wealth nor power can assure the scintillating productivity that we so much admire in the cases of Athens and Florence.

Another position of Vygotsky's, to which I felt powerfully drawn, has to do with the connection he saw between teaching and mental development. In contrast to Piaget, who seemed to ignore completely the effects his observational and interviewing techniques may have had on the mental behavior of the children he is describing, Vygotsky stressed the interconnectedness of the mode of experimental or pedagogical intervention and the resultant development of the mind of the child. This reminded me of Heisenberg's indeterminacy principle — that there is no way a particle can be observed without disturbing it.[1] Our knowledge of things can be only our knowledge of how they act as a result of our observing and experimenting with them. For if the child's mind "as it truly is" cannot be that mind at rest and undisturbed, then we must face up to and accept the dramatic alternative: The child's mind is likewise defined by how it acts when probed and stimulated by countless forms of intervention. If, then, the child's mind realizes itself as the result of a variety of pedagogical interventions, then teaching and mental development cannot be severed from one another. To paraphrase Vygotsky, the only good teaching is that which stays ahead of development and draws it up behind.[2] Moreover, if the child's cognitive performance is a function of the teacher's pedagogical performance, then we must find ways of greatly expanding the teacher's capacity for challenging the child to respond. There was, in all of this it seemed to me, a clear call for a curriculum far beyond the power of the typical classroom teacher to construct — a curriculum representing an enormous discipline dedicated to unsettling the mind and forcing it to come to grips with what it might otherwise take complacently for granted. The conclusions I found in Vygotsky's *Thought and Language* (1962) and *Mind in Society* (1978) showed me how to apply, specifically to the relationship between teaching and mental development, the views I had arrived at earlier as a result of repeatedly dipping into Pierce and Dewey, as well as more sustained examinations of Buchler's *Toward a General Theory of Human Judgment* (1951) and *Nature and Judgment* (1955).

When I first read Vygotsky, in the late 1940s, I was unprepared for his strong emphasis on the connection between thinking and language. I was still caught up in the social behaviorism of American pragmatism, which inclined me to favor the stress on interaction with the environment that I found in Piaget. The philosophy and psychology of language did not seem to me to have the glamorous patina that they were later to develop. I read psychology during those years because I enjoyed doing so, even though my chosen field was philosophy. While I found

Vygotsky to be, for the most part, quite congenial, I was far more fascinated by the social psychology of George Herbert Mead, to whose works (written in the first third of the 20th century) I had been introduced by Professor Herbert Schneider.

If Dewey's work extended to the farthest reaches of pragmatic experimentalism, Mead's seemed to me to be at its very core. I saw — and still see — no conflict between them: They simply approached different areas of interest with much the same method. Mead's chief area of interest was the genesis of community through communication and of the thinking self through internationalization of that community. (I can still remember stopping Professor Schneider in the corridor of Columbia University's Philosophy Hall and exclaiming that I had discovered "the source" of Mead's ideas — not Hegel, I argued, but the obscure nineteenth-century French philosopher-psychologist Maine de Biran. Schneider seemed pleased.)

In the years that followed, I considered myself to be a Mead enthusiast, having been strongly impressed by his *Mind, Self and Society*. But I was also, from even further back, a disciple of John Dewey.

I had been introduced to Dewey (and to his wife and two young adopted children) by Lyle Eddy. Dewey was then about 90. As his hearing aid did not seem to be working well, he was content (after inquiring about what the children had had for breakfast) to talk for the two-hour visit; we were more than content to listen. I didn't try to tell him about how committed I already was to his way of thinking — so committed, in fact, that I had traveled with Patton's infantry through Germany during World War II with a copy of Dewey's *Intelligence in the Modern World* (1939) stowed away in my backpack. Subsequently we had some correspondence, and two years later Dewey's long life (I recall his saying that the earliest part of it seemed to him to belong to someone else) came to a close.

At the time I became involved with education, in the late 1960s, I still hadn't read much of Dewey's educational writings, although I think I had more or less deduced his pedagogy from related convictions he had expressed in such works as *Human Nature and Conduct* (1922), *Art as Experience* (1934), and *Experience and Nature* (1929/1958). Doubtless, there is no one "right" way to read Dewey, but the method I happened to employ, of reading the major noneducational works first, seems to me far more felicitous than reading the pedagogical works first — or reading only those works.

I saw myself eventually putting these various educational theories into practice. I am referring to the notion I took from Dewey that an educational session should begin with *an experience* — a unified, cognitive/

affective event that would both provoke and sustain continued reflection by the class. I refer, also, to the idea I took from Dewey and Mead that the school had to harness and put to work the social impulses of the child — in contrast to the imperial, divide-and-rule strategy that some teachers even today still employ. The central thrust of the educational revolution to come — the thrust pioneered by Dewey and Vygotsky — was the insistence on the primacy of thinking rather than of knowledge in education.

When, in the late 1960s, I decided to try a new approach to the elementary school curriculum, I had sympathy with Dewey's recommendation that each discipline be reconstructed into a form of scientific inquiry so that each student could become an inquirer. Nevertheless, it was my hunch that children were primarily intent on obtaining meaning — this is why they so often condemned school as meaningless — and wanted meanings they could verbalize. It was here that scientific inquiry was less promising than philosophical inquiry. I saw philosophy as the discipline par excellence for making sense of things and for preparing students to think in the more specific disciplines. And yet the experience of teachers with traditional, academic philosophy had been anything but satisfactory. Philosophy might be indispensable for the redesign of education, but to make this happen it would itself have to be redesigned. It would have to be a brighter, more readable version of philosophy, in which the great ideas would continue to sparkle yet would provide, as nothing else can, the much needed strengthening of children's reasoning, concept-formation abilities, and judgment.

I shall skip over the years that have intervened since I first tried to envisage what a children's community of inquiry might be like, the result of which was *Harry Stottlemeier's Discovery* (Lipman, 1974). I pick the story up again in 1989, 20 years later. Philosophy for Children is now virtually complete as a curriculum and is a member of the National Diffusion Network (NDN). Dr. Lee Wickline, the longtime director of NDN, had been approached by Dr. Nikolai Nikandrov, Deputy Director of the USSR's Academy of Pedagogical Sciences (APS). Dr. Nikandrov said that Soviet schools were in trouble: The students complained that what they were being taught was irrelevant and the school system had no way of identifying and supporting the superior academic programs that might provide Soviet children with a more meaningful education. Dr. Wickline visited Moscow to discuss the matter further — this was in the summer of 1989 — and was asked to follow up that visit with further visits from content specialists, particularly in the area of critical thinking. I was asked if I would be interested in going, and I immediately accepted. Before long, I had an invitation from APS to visit for three weeks. I replied that I could stay only for four days, but it was agreed that such a quick visit might nevertheless be profitable.

In advance of my visit, I sent the APS some materials dealing with Philosophy for Children, which I consider the critical thinking approach that has the greatest range and depth for children at the elementary school level. I also sent a few chapters of *Pixie* (Lipman, 1981), a philosophical novel for 9- and 10-year-olds, which I asked to have translated into Russian. This is the sequence of events over the next few days as I remember them:

Sunday, October 7. I meet, after dinner, with Dr. Vitaly Rubtsov (who is a close associate of Dr. Davydov) and Dr. Arkady Margolis, both of the APS staff, as well as with a number of other psychologists, to discuss the schedule of the next two days. Although I speak no Russian, they all speak English and we get along quite well. But, as yet, we have hardly touched on any substantive issues.

Monday, October 8. I pay a visit, along with the APS group, to Moscow School #91 and conduct a session on *Pixie* with fourth graders. Despite the awkwardness of having to translate everything said in English into Russian and vice versa, the dialogue moves along very nicely and productively. For example, we discuss Pixie's claim to be writing the story of how she wrote her "mystery story." I ask the children if their desks have stories, if their school has a story, if their country has a story, and if the world has a story. To each they assent, with some elaboration. (Afterwards, I regretted not having asked them whether the history of the world was its story or the story of its story.) I conclude the exercise by asking them if they, too, have stories. To this, they enthusiastically agree. At the end of the session, to my surprise and delight, a number of them come forward to ask if I would like them to write their stories of themselves so that they could give them to me. This offer of reciprocity — in which I begin the session by offering them my story and they conclude the session by offering me theirs — represents precisely the kind of meaningful exchange to be expected of a community of inquiry, although I myself am quite surprised to have it happen after only a single meeting.

Another feature of the session worth noting has to do with the way the dialogue develops. The aim of a community of inquiry is to move from teacher–student dialogue to student–student dialogue. I was a bit afraid, before the session began, that this movement might be inhibited by the need to filter all discussion through the interpreter. But, from the start, the discussion is animated and there are lots of hands in the air. Soon the device of funneling all the conversation through the interpreter becomes so objectionable to the students that they short-circuit me and develop numerous discussions among themselves. And so they end up doing what I had hoped they would do, although by a quite unexpected route.

After dinner that evening, we look at the BBC film on Philosophy for Children, which I have brought on cassette. (Interestingly, the other two one-hour films in the three-part BBC series also have connections with Vygotsky's work.) Subsequently, we discuss a two-page memorandum that I had prepared the previous week, entitled "Forming a Philosophical Community of Inquiry."

The memorandum was written after I had read Dr. Davydov's most recent book, *Problems of Developmental Teaching* (he wrote it in 1986), as serialized in *Soviet Psychology*. My memorandum was an attempt to unpack the sequence of psychological events that took place in a session of Philosophy for Children, such as the one that was enacted at School #91 that morning. I paid particular attention to such Vygotskyan concepts as "internalization" and "appropriation," showing how they were realized as the dialogue unfolded. I also showed the compatibility or similarity between Philosophy for Children practice and the pedagogical theory of Professor Davydov.

Tuesday, October 9. The day begins with another *Pixie* session in School #91. It seems to me that it goes equally well. When the discussion turns to thoughts and I ask if all one's thoughts need to be supported by reasons, one girl remarks, "Only those you express; not those you think." Another girl tells me that relationships can themselves have relationships. She and several other students then proceed to construct an analogy as an illustration of this point.

After lunch, as we walk on the sidewalk along one of Moscow's enormous boulevards, Dr. Rubtsov and I discuss the next steps to be taken: the exchange visits, the exchange of conferences, the appointment of APS as the USSR affiliate center of the Institute for the Advancement of Philosophy for Children (IAPC) and so on.

Later that afternoon, we meet with the APS Vice President, Professor Davydov. He has apparently been well briefed about the demonstrations I provided and the progress of the various discussions that had taken place. He quickly assents to the preparation of a joint agreement or protocol, which he and I sign. We chat a bit longer, then the three-quarters-of-an-hour visit is over and the following day I leave Moscow, bound for London.

I cannot help thinking that we have shown the feasibility of welding together the chief variety of Soviet educational psychology with one particular variety of American educational practice. But why hadn't the Soviet psychologists thought of our approach themselves?

The answer, I suspect, is to be found in an unwarranted presupposition very prevalent among educators in all countries (not just in the Soviet Union). This presupposition is that what must be avoided at all cost is the introduction of another subject into the elementary school curriculum. Instead, each discipline is expected to cultivate and enhance the thinking that takes place in its own bailiwick. This means that the new thinking activities to be introduced must be virtually transparent or "content-free."

What is overlooked in this approach is the fact that content-free materials are also meaning-free and that children are hungry for meaning. There is, however, one discipline that specializes in meanings, in values, in concepts, in reasonings, in the making of judgments (both evaluational and classificatory), and that is philosophy. The addition of philosophy to the curriculum of the schools is a drastic step, but not more drastic than the dire situation we are in demands. Perhaps the reason the Soviets could make such a swift decision is that they are not bewildered by countless alternatives, for each of which there are countless momentary enthusiasms, extensive claims, and virtually no theoretical support. It seems to me they knew what would count as a successful implementation of their theoretical position and they recognized it as soon as they perceived it in operation. In the end, they may settle on some as yet unthought of alternative, but if that happens it will be to a considerable extent because Philosophy for Children has opened their eyes to the educational solution that their theory makes possible and that is almost within their grasp.

I cannot close without mentioning that none of this would have been possible just a few short years ago. For more than 40 years the writings of Vygotsky were proscribed in the USSR and those who considered themselves his followers were, for at least part of this time, barred from holding positions of educational authority. All of that is now changed. Professors Davydov and Rubtsov are now firmly in the saddle. It will be interesting to see in which direction they choose to go.

NOTES

1. Werner Heisenberg was a German physicist whose theory of quantum mechanics won him a Nobel prize in 1932.
2. See Vygotsky (trans. 1962); see also Vygotsky's *Thinking and Speech*, in Vygotsky (trans. 1987), Vol. 1, p. 212.

CHRONOLOGY OF
PHILOSOPHY FOR CHILDREN

Before proceeding to *Natasha*, I have to take into account the fact that most readers will have little idea of Philosophy for Children as an enterprise. They will have little familiarity with how it works, even assuming that they are already familiar with traditional academic philosophy. And they will have little knowledge of its development, the stages by which it has come to be. I therefore offer a time line that indicates the dates of publication of the components of the curriculum as well as other details that might be helpful to the reader wishing to get a sense of the scope of Philosophy for Children as well as of its historical record.

1969   Writing of first book in Philosophy for Children curriculum: *Harry Stottlemeier's Discovery* (*Harry*) — for ages 11–12 — with the support of the National Endowment for the Humanities (NEH).

1970   Offset printing of approximately 350 copies of *Harry* and conducting of experiment at the Rand School (Montclair Public Schools), both with the help of a grant from the NEH.

1973   Organization and holding of conference in "Pre-College Philosophy" at Montclair State College (MSC).

1974   Establishment of IAPC as part of MSC.

        Publication by IAPC of *Harry* thanks to a grant from the Brand Foundation. Announcement of the existence of the children's book, the establishment of the IAPC, and the results of an experiment at a session of the Eastern Division of the American Philosophical Association's (APA) annual conference.

1975   Writing (together with Ann Margaret Sharp and Frederick S. Oscanyan) of first edition of *Philosophical Inquiry*, the instructional manual to accompany *Harry*.

Conducting of teacher-education project in Newark, at Miller Street and Morton Street Schools, with support from the NEH.

Conference in Philosophy for Children, held at Rutgers University Continuing Education Center, New Brunswick, with support from the New Jersey Committee for the Humanities.

1976   Award of five-year development grant from New Jersey Department of Education (Title IV-C) to develop test of children's reasoning.

Holding of five- to seven-day workshop/conferences to train professors of philosophy to prepare teachers to foster children's critical and creative thinking. Sites: Rutgers (New Brunswick), Fordham, Yale, and Harvard. Aided by NEH, Fordham, Rockefeller, and Schultz Foundation grants.

Publication by IAPC of first edition of *Philosophical Inquiry*, with support from Schumann Foundation.

Publication by IAPC of first edition of *Lisa*, an ethics reader for children ages 12–13.

1977   Publication by IAPC of first edition of *Ethical Inquiry*, instructional manual to accompany *Lisa*.

Publication by IAPC of first edition of *Philosophy in the Classroom*.

Holding of five- to seven-day workshop/conferences for professors of philosophy. Sites: Michigan State University, University of Illinois at Champaign–Urbana, and Albion College.

Beginning of in-service teacher education programs in New Jersey and a few other states.

1978   Publication by Temple University Press of *Growing Up with Philosophy*.

Publication by IAPC of *Suki*, for children ages 14–15.

Publication by IAPC of *Mark*, for secondary school students.

Development of *Thinking About Thinking*, a five-part filmstrip aimed at assisting the teaching with the logic portion of *Harry*.

Completion of experiment sponsored by New Jersey Department of Education and carried out under auspices of Educational Testing Service. Sites: Newark and Pompton Lakes, New Jersey.

Award by Rockefeller Foundation of three-year Research Scholar grant.

Beginning of utilization of Pocono Environmental Education Center in Dingman's Falls, Pennsylvania, for the purpose of training future teacher educators, as well as for summer teacher-education workshops.

1979   Publication of Vol. 1, No. 1 of *Thinking: The Journal of Philosophy For Children*.

Publication by IAPC of *Mark*, for children ages 16–17.

1980   Publication by IAPC of *Social Inquiry*, manual to accompany *Mark*.

Publication by Temple University Press of second edition of *Philosophy in the Classroom*.

Publication by IAPC of *Writing: How and Why*, manual to accompany *Suki*.

Publication by Harvard University Press of *Philosophy and the Young Child* by Gareth B. Matthews.

1981   Completion of Educational Testing Service (ETS) one-year experiment—a study of 4,500 New Jersey students in 10 demographically diverse communities, under direction of ETS Senior Research Psychologist, Dr. Virginia Shipman.

Holding of International Conference for Teacher Educators in Philosophy for Children, MSC.

Publication by IAPC of *Pixie*, for children ages 9–10.

1982   Award of three-year research grant by Schumann Foundation.

Publication by IAPC of *Kio and Gus*, for children ages 9–10.

Publication by IAPC of *Looking for Meaning*, instructional manual to accompany *Pixie*.

1983   Publication by Arden Press of Ronald Reed's *Talking with Children*.

Completion of *New Jersey Test of Reasoning*.

Publication of second edition of *Lisa* by IAPC.

1984   Publication by IAPC of revised edition of *Philosophical Inquiry*.

Publication by IAPC of *New Jersey Test of Reasoning*.

Formation at MSC of International Council for Elementary and Secondary School Philosophy as well as the Center for Cognitive Growth in Early Childhood, both of which were short-lived predecessors of the International Council for Philosophical Inquiry with Children (ICPIC).

Publication by Harvard University Press of *Dialogues with Children* by Gareth Matthews.

1985 Publication by IAPC of second edition of *Ethical Inquiry*.

Publication by University Press of America of *Philosophical Adventures with Children* by Michael Pritchard.

Founding of ICPIC following one of the first workshops for the training of trainers held outside the United States. This one was held in Denmark. (Subsequent ICPIC conferences have been held in Spain, Austria, Brazil, Mexico, and China.)

Discontinuation of use of Pocono Environmental Education Center for training of trainers and beginning of utilization instead of St. Marguerite's Retreat House in Mendham, New Jersey, for one 10-day and two two-week sessions each year.

Beginning of Master's Program in Teaching Philosophy to Children at MSC.

1986 Philosophy for Children designated a "meritorious educational program" by the National Diffusion Network of the U.S. Department of Education and given annually renewable dissemination support.

Publication by IAPC of *Wondering at the World*, instructional manual to accompany *Kio and Gus*.

1987 Publication by IAPC of *Elfie*, for children ages 6–8.

1988 Publication by Temple University Press of *Philosophy Goes to School*.

Publication by IAPC of *Getting Our Thoughts Together*, instructional manual to accompany *Elfie*.

Establishment at MSC of Institute for Critical Thinking (ICT).

1989 Beginnings of support by ICT of IAPC through the funding of fellowships for Visiting Scholars and assistantships for master's students.

1990   BBC produces *Socrates for Six-Year-Olds*, a one-hour film on Philosophy for Children, and shows it in Britain, the United States, Japan, Israel, and other countries around the world.

1991   Publication by Cambridge University Press of *Thinking in Education*.

        Publication by Kendall/Hunt of *Children in Chaos* by Leonard Harris.

1992   Publication by Temple University Press of *Studies in Philosophy for Children: Harry Stottlemeier's Discovery*.

1993   Publication by Kendall/Hunt of *Thinking Children and Education*.

        Publication of *Thinking Stories*, Vol. 1, ed. by Phil Cam (Australia).

1994   Publication of *Thinking Stories*, Vol. 2, ed. by Phil Cam (Australia).

        Reissue (in paperback) by Kendall/Hunt of *Growing Up With Philosophy*.

        Publication by Harvard University Press of *The Philosophy of Childhood* by Gareth Matthews.

1995   Montclair State College becomes Montclair State University (MSU). Philosophy for Children revalidated by National Diffusion Network. Doctoral programs in Philosophy for Children begin to make their appearance.

The foregoing chronicle is severely limited. It deals primarily with English-language publications, and it ignores, for the most part, events in countries other than the United States. Thus, it does not list the annual or biannual conferences of the ICPIC; it makes little or no mention of foreign publications and regional, as opposed to international, conferences; it does not allude to the development of an international cadre of certified teacher educators. But some sense of the centrifugal force of the elementary school philosophy movement can be gained by considering that there are presently 40 affiliate centers around the world engaging in teacher education, curriculum development, and/or education research. And the IAPC curriculum has, as of the mid-1990s, been translated, partially or completely, into 20 languages.

NATASHA

FIRST VISIT

The phone rings. Natasha something-or-other; I can't tell what the last name is because of the unmistakable Russian accent. A reporter. She wants to interview me for a project she is working on. We quickly set a date and time.

I am pleased with the idea. My wife, Teri, and I had visited Moscow the previous month, and had met with some of the officials in the Academy of Pedagogical Sciences. At the end of the visit, we had signed an agreement to cooperate through future exchanges, leading toward the Soviets eventually undertaking to experiment with the Philosophy for Children program and perhaps even to consider utilizing it in some of their schools.

When the reporter arrives, I say, "I didn't quite catch your name. You're Russian?"

"No, I'm Ukrainian." So much for the "unmistakable Russian accent" hypothesis. She spells out her last name, her voice faintly betraying impatience. "You wouldn't happen to have some coffee, would you?"

"I was just about to ask you if you wanted some. I'll be right back." We seem to be on different wavelengths.

She dismisses the croissant with an almost imperious gesture, lights a cigarette, frowns, and begins, "Let me tell you why I'm here. I read about your negotiations with the APS, and I thought it might be something I could do an article, or a series of articles, about."

"You're on the staff of a Soviet educational journal?"

"No, I'm one of the new breed of journalistic entrepreneurs. I'm freelance." I do not comment, so she continues, "Let me come to the point. I'm interested in knowing what you see that interests you in our educational theory."

"It's a question I've asked myself many times," I say. "So I'm doubly glad you're interested in possibly doing a story. It will help move things along in Russia."

"Maybe," she says. "Maybe not." Her momentary, wintry smile disquiets me, as it was evidently meant to do.

"Whatever," I add. "And besides, it would be helpful to me to have someone to talk with who is knowledgeable about these things."

3

The deadpan stare evokes a fugitive association with the Ninotchka of Garbo. I remark, "You have a background in education, I take it."

"I did my dissertation on Vygotsky and I have studied with Davydov. I have taught in the primary school and in the university. What's novel for me is being a reporter."

"You dropped out of academic life of your own volition?"

The frosty glance again. "I'm supposed to be interviewing you, not you me."

"That's just it!" I exclaim. "I need to interview you also! It should be reciprocal!"

She looks at me soberly. "I don't know," she says slowly, "it defeats the whole purpose of the traditional interview format. I need to be impersonal, even self-effacing. I need you to have confidence in my neutrality and objectivity. A reciprocal interview? Ugh! The idea is completely unacceptable! What would happen? I'd ask you your age and you'd ask me mine! Don't you see — it would never work!"

I peer at her as mildly as I can. "But you were prepared to interview me, and in so doing to describe me, treating me as an object so as to display me to your readers, am I not right? But you balk when I suggest that it be reciprocal."

She reddens just a bit. "That's right. I'm not used to being taken by surprise." A small smile plays at the corners of her mouth. "It's probably a totally unworkable idea, but let's try it."

She turns on her tape recorder and I turn on mine.

*   *   *   *

"And so," she says, taking up her notebook, "how should we begin?"

"Where did you plan to begin?"

"I was going to start out by asking you what you expected to accomplish by going to Moscow."

"I guess that's as good a place to begin as any. I went at the suggestion of Lee Wickline, Director of the Schools Effectiveness Division of the U.S. Department of Education. He said the Soviets were interested in talking with a content specialist in the area of critical thinking."

Natasha sighs faintly and repeats her question, "What did you expect to accomplish?" She lights another cigarette and waves the match vigorously in the air until it goes out. "I hope you don't mind my smoking," she remarks, half as a question and half as a defiant assertion.

"I'd prefer you didn't, frankly," I manage to say, and she quickly stubs it out. The smoke lingers in the silence that follows. "As for what I'd hoped to accomplish, I don't think I had a clear picture of that when the possibility of the trip first came up. It was only gradually that I began to realize that this might be an exceptional opportunity."

"An opportunity for what?"

"To visit a country in response to an official invitation and demonstrate to them that the *practice* of *our* educational approach was completely consistent with *their* educational *theory*. In fact, I thought I could show them that our program better operationalized *their* theoretical understanding of education than anything *they* could come up with."

"Did you tell them that?"

"No, of course not. All I asked them to do for me was to translate two or three short chapters from one of our novels for 10-year-olds and to arrange for me to teach a group of such children."

"Did you attempt to explain to them in advance what you planned to do?"

"No, I'm afraid I didn't. One of the psychologists even said to me, rather anxiously, just before the first session with the children, 'You're going to *inspire* them, aren't you?' I answered him with a curt 'No.' If I'd had time, I would have added, 'Just the opposite. I intend to be as self-effacing as possible. The teacher is needed as a mediator, of course, but the primary mediator is the story itself. The role of the teacher can perhaps be better described as that of a facilitator.'"

As I speak, Natasha is writing away furiously in her notebook. Then she straightens up and remarks, "So do you see this as a point of disagreement between your approach and the Vygotsky/Davydov approach?"

I stare out the window of my office. The office itself is on the ground floor of the IAPC on the campus of MSC (now MSU) in New Jersey. The Institute is actually a wood-frame, three-story house, converted from a private dwelling. The two windows in my office look out over a small backyard, a garage, a tiny grove of trees, and the larger backyard of the house of the president of the college. Behind the garage, the leafless trees, like an intricate overlay of conceptual art, break up the morose November sky into countless jagged fragments.

"Not so much a point of disagreement as a point of amplification," I observe. "They tend to put all the burden of mediation on the teacher, and I say that's overburdening the teacher. Besides, it's misplaced. The major burden of mediation should be borne by the text."

Natasha puts her notebook on the low, oval table, closes her eyes momentarily, utters a sigh of despair, then scowls at me. "This is the wrong way to begin. Absolutely the wrong way. We are getting nowhere. All of a sudden, out of nowhere, we're talking about mediation. Who knows anything of what Vygotsky and Davydov mean by mediation? At this point, no one. We can't just start talking about mediation in — in —"

"*In media res.*"

"Thanks a lot!" she says crisply. "In my opinion, what we need to do first is establish some guidelines — some procedural rules so that we won't be trying to deal with everything all at once."

"Fine!" I exclaim. "And as I see it, that's precisely what you've just started us doing, by stipulating that we should try to take things up in a logical order, not in any which way. But that brings me to *my* point, which is, what are the things we're talking about? We need — don't we? — an agenda of some sort?"

She nods. "The agenda would provide the substance and the rules would provide the procedure. Fair enough." For the moment, she seems content. The very next moment she turns on me. "What are we waiting for?" she storms.

"I think we can begin by discussing the items to be on the agenda, and as we do so, the rules we need to observe will emerge more or less of their own accord." I say this in a measured, deliberate sort of way, and my tone evidently sets her teeth on edge.

"Please don't speak to me the way a male academic speaks to a student," she says in a steely voice. "That's one of the reasons I left my position in the university! If we're truly going to be engaged here in reciprocal research, then let's treat each other with respect, as equals, all right?"

"I wasn't trying to preempt the role of reasonableness —" I begin, but she quickly interrupts: "Enough! I've had my say! Let's get on with it. Let me tell you what I see as the first thing I need to know."

"Okay, what's that?"

"What do you know about Soviet educational psychology in the twentieth century? I mean, what have you read?"

"Not all that much, I'm afraid. I've read Vygotsky's *Thought and Language* as well as his *Mind in Society*. I've read the major portion of Davydov's *Problems of Developmental Teaching*. And I've dipped into a good portion of Amonashvili's *Hello Children*, although that's a work I really don't want to discuss."

"Why not?" Natasha asks innocently, thereby managing to get me to do precisely what I have just proclaimed I don't want to do.

"Because it's a throwback to the affective education of the 1960s, to A.S. Neill's *Summerhill*, and to the Woodstock generation. It stresses the ethical and creative sides of education but neglects the critical side. It's a fragment of truth masquerading as the whole truth. I can see why Soviet printers can't keep up with the demand for Amonashvili's "humanistic education" approach and why Western educators flock to attend his conferences in Georgia. But the problem is to make education cognitive as well as affective, critical as well as creative, social as well as individual, and so on." I pause and then add, lamely, "You've made me give a speech."

"I didn't make you do anything you didn't already want to do." The discussion comes to a standstill. "Your plants seem to be thriving," she observes at last.

"They get plenty of light," I reply.

She arches her eyebrows. "Let's get back to my question. What do you know about twentieth-century educational psychology in the USSR?"

"To tell the truth, the picture I have of it comes mostly from Davydov. I see a line of development that starts in the 1920s and is composed of five segments. In the first segment, all by himself, is Vygotsky. In the second group are those who worked with him or were his immediate followers, like Luria, Leont'ev, and Rubinstein. Third come those who may not have had a direct connection with Vygotsky, but who in any event had an influence on Davydov. Here I'm thinking of such people as El'konin and Il'enkov, as well as Gal'perin and Zaporozhets. In the fourth group, which is headed by Davydov himself, are all those who worked with him in his 25 years of experimentation in School #91 as well as those whose independent research had an important impact on his thinking. I mean people like Zak, Kapterev, Shimina, Minskaia, and Makhmutov. Finally, there are the younger colleagues of Davydov, like Rubstov and Margolis. How about it? Am I far off base?"

Natasha shrugs and avoids my question. "What about Skatkin?" she inquires.

"Ah, yes! Skatkin! Absolutely. Davydov takes his work very seriously, and from what I learned of it through Davydov's book, it seems to be excellent. But of course I'm partial to people who have a background in philosophy, as Vygotsky and Davydov do, and as I suspect Skatkin has also."

"You're making a lot of suppositions."

"Yes, but it's just my impression of the personnel that have been involved in developing the theoretical position that has descended from Vygotsky."

"Well, all right, we'll let that stand for the time being. What about you? Where do you come from — intellectually, I mean."

"For me, the pivotal figure has always been Dewey. Earlier than

Dewey, of course, there was the founder of the American school, Charles Peirce. And then, alongside Dewey, there was George Herbert Mead. Subsequently, there was the generation that formed a bridge between Dewey's era and my own, a generation that included professors such as Columbia University's renowned professor of art history, Meyer Schapiro, thought by many to be the most brilliant faculty member on campus, John Herman Randall, Jr., a redoubtable historian of philosophy, and Ernest Nagel, everywhere respected for his work in the methodology of science. There was still another bridge: Justus Buchler, who was 10 years older than I was, and the author of a number of profound metaphysical studies."

"But these were people you knew directly," she says, "or were connected with people you knew directly. What about other influences?"

I give a quick nod of agreement. "Right, such people as Simmel, Weber, Durkheim, as Paul Schilder, as Jean-Paul Sartre and Gaston Bachelard and Maurice Merleau-Ponty. And, later, Austin, Ryle, and Wittgenstein." Then I add, "I didn't really get interested in linguistic analysis until everyone else was beginning to think of leaving it as a sinking ship. What I saw in it, particularly its interest in mental acts, was its potential for sharpening children's cognitive skills."

We seem to have reached a transition point in our talk, having worked through the last point and beginning now to touch on something else. I suggest a break, perhaps a walk about the campus, and Natasha assents, although with no diminution of her usual solemnity.

*   *   *   *

Our stroll takes us first to a bit of a ridge, a hundred steps or so from the Institute, from which we can see, from a dozen or so miles away, the whole gorgeous sweep of the skyline of Manhattan. Natasha nods, but remains skeptical and uncommunicative.

"What we're standing on," I tell her, "is what is known as 'First Mountain.' It's a result of the readjustment of the earth's crust that formed the Palisades and the channel for the Hudson River. Between here and there are the Jersey meadows. This ridge runs for miles in a north–south direction, precisely parallel to Manhattan. It provides us in New Jersey with a magnificent view of the city."

Natasha frowns. "Look, I don't want you to have any misconceptions," she says slowly. "You say what we're doing is reciprocal, but in my mind there are two separate inquiries going on. You are trying to understand the intellectual sources of the Philosophy for Children program, and I'm trying to understand what you're doing and how you're doing it."

"Fair enough," I tell her, "but what misconception am I in danger of forming?"

"That my job is to correct you when you're wrong, or to verify what you say when you're right. For example, I have my own ideas about what Vygotsky is all about: I've already expressed those ideas in my thesis. I'm not interested in doing further research on Vygotsky, or in doing joint research with you on Davydov. You have your inquiry and I have mine. The difference is that your inquiry is the subject of my inquiry, but mine is not the subject of yours."

We walk on, and I point out to her the campus version of a Greek amphitheater—a gem, I explain, but placed so close to the busy road-way as to be virtually useless. She glances at it impatiently and says, "Do you agree?"

"Of course! But I would put it this way. Together we form a dyad, a single community of inquiry. It is an inquiry, however, that demands complex thinking, and complex thinking, as I would define it, is think-ing that takes into account its own methodology or procedures all the while that it is dealing with its purported subject-matter."

Her face lightens a bit. "Okay! Okay! So we have a single inquiry, with a division of labor. You proceed to study whatever it is you want to study—"

"I will follow my inquiry wherever it leads—"

"Right, and I will study how you go about it. You can say, if you like, that it's a single inquiry with a division of labor, but I prefer to think that what I'm doing is a kind of meta-level research, a meta-inquiry."

"And look," I point out, "we're generating our own rules of proce-dure, just as I said we would!"

She looks at me soberly, with just a hint of mockery in her eyes. "Don't get too self-congratulatory," she remarks. "The hard part is yet to come." She hangs fire for a moment. "There's this 'community of inquiry' thing."

"What about it?"

"What is it?"

Our walk has taken us to the little plaza in front of the sprawling, white student center building. It's too chilly to stay for long; neverthe-less, we take advantage of the availability of the bench nearest us, and I begin a rather elaborate exposition: "Look, let's say we agree on our goal, which is the improvement of student thinking. By that I mean getting students to think more creatively and more critically, which is what higher-order thinking involves. Now the only way we can get at the thinking is to get at its source or matrix, which is dialogue—"

"Dialogical thinking, verbal thinking, this is the only kind of thinking you recognize?" she comments dubiously.

"No, of course not," I exclaim impatiently. "There are lots of other kinds of thinking—in symbols other than words, and in actions, like making and doing. But in the context of the school, where the emphasis is on knowing and reasoning and analyzing, we can get the greatest leverage if we emphasize verbal thinking. And, of course, that is what most children expect to have to emphasize, too."

"So dialogue is the matrix of thinking, and you encourage dialogue by teaching children to discuss philosophy in the classroom."

I look up at the sky and tap my fingers on my knee. "Sorry," she says. "Go on."

"To foster discourse," I proceed to explain, "there needs to be a discursive community. But the ordinary class does not know how to convert itself into such a community, so we first have to draw them a picture—no, that's not the right way to put it—we first have to show them a model of a fictional community of inquiry and trust that they will more or less instinctively begin to emulate the model. I'm getting chilly. Let's go back to the Institute, what d'you say?"

She nods, stands, and we walk silently alongside the mall. "I'm sorry about that," I say, after a minute or two has gone by. "I overreact, sometimes, when I hear people speak of 'teaching philosophy to children' as if it were the height of absurdity—some sort of howler that perfectly illustrates the ridiculous lengths to which some ivory tower professors will go to put their theories into practice."

Natasha does not allow herself to be sidetracked into a discussion of my pet irritabilities. "Is this the way you explained the community of inquiry to the psychologists at the APS in Moscow?"

"No," I admit, somewhat chastened by her businesslike attitude and her refusal to explore the beckoning byways of unreasonableness. "I gave them a two-page outline, and we reviewed it line by line."

"May I see it?"

"As soon as we get back to the Institute."

For the most part, I keep my papers in six large filing drawers located close by my desk, and I file them myself. This is why they are readily available when I can remember where I put them, and why no one can help me when I can't remember. In this instance, I have no trouble finding what I was looking for, and I hand Natasha a copy without further comment. This is it:

FORMING A PHILOSOPHICAL COMMUNITY OF INQUIRY

I. Presentation of the Text
   1. The text as a model, in story form, of a community of inquiry
   2. The text as reflecting the values and achievements of past generations
   3. The text as mediator between the culture and the individual
   4. The text as a highly peculiar object of perception that carries mental reflection already within itself
   5. The portraying of human relationships as possibly analyzable in terms of logical relations (e.g., reciprocity, transitivity, symmetry, etc.)
   6. Taking turns reading aloud
      a. The ethical implications of alternating reading and listening
      b. The oral reproduction of the written text
      c. Turn-taking as a division of labor: the beginnings of classroom community
   7. Gradual internalization of the thinking behaviors of the fictional characters (e.g., reading how a fictional character asks a question may lead a real child to ask such a question in class)
   8. Discovery by the class that the text is meaningful and relevant, and the appropriation by the members of the class of those meanings
II. The Construction of the Agenda
   1. The offering of questions: the initial response of the class to the text
   2. Recognition by the teacher of the names of the contributing individuals
   3. The construction of the agenda as a collaborative work of the community
   4. The agenda as a map of areas of student interest
   5. The agenda as an index of what students consider important in the text and as an expression of the group's cognitive needs
   6. Cooperation of teacher and students in deciding where to begin the discussion
   7. Discovery of the problematic — of discrepancies, inconsistencies, and contradictions to be overcome by the process of inquiry
III. Solidifying the Community
   1. Group solidarity through dialogical inquiry
   2. The primacy of activity over reflection

3. The articulation of disagreements and the quest for understanding
4. Fostering cognitive skills (e.g., assumption-finding, generalization, exemplification) through dialogical practice
5. Learning to employ cognitive tools (e.g., reasons, criteria,
concepts, algorithms, rules, principles)
6. Joining together in cooperative reasoning (e.g., building on
each other's ideas, offering counterexamples or alternative
hypotheses, etc.)
7. Internalization of the overt cognitive behavior of the community (e.g., introjecting the ways in which one's classmates
correct one another until one becomes systematically self-
corrective) — "intrapsychical reproduction of the interpsychical"
8. Becoming increasingly sensitive to meaningful nuances of con-
textual differences
9. Group collectively "gropes its way" along, following the argument where it leads; deliberations proceed toward settlements
(judgments)
IV. Using Exercises and Discussion Plans
1. Employing questions from the academic tradition: recourse to
professional guidance
2. Appropriation by the students of the methodology of the discipline
3. Opening students to other philosophical alternatives
4. Focusing on specific problems so as to compel the making of
practical judgments; ascending from relations to relationships
5. Compelling the inquiry to examine overarching regulative
ideas such as truth, community, personhood, beauty, justice,
and goodness
V. Encouraging Further Responses
1. Eliciting further responses (in the form of the telling or writing
of stories, poetry, painting, drawing, and other forms of cognitive expression)
2. Recognizing the synthesis of the critical and the creative with
the individual and the communal
3. Celebrating the deepened sense of meaning that comes with
strengthened judgment

Natasha studies the document silently, frowning as she reads certain portions, but nodding in agreement as she comes to others. Finally,
when she asks, "I can keep this, no?", it is my turn to nod in agreement.
She then proceeds to peruse the outline a second time, but this time

jumping about from section to section, examining some more intently than others. Finally, she asks me — or, more precisely, orders me — to obtain my own copy so that we could review matters together.

"I can see why the psychologists at APS might find this of some interest," she says slowly. She sits for a moment with her mouth pursed, staring at the first page. Then she asks, "Could you tell me more about part I, item 5? For example, is there any significance to the fact that you begin by talking about 'relationships' and end by referring to 'relations'?"

I can't help grinning at what she had first picked out. "One of John Dewey's last works," I say, "written with Arthur Bentley and published when Dewey was 90, was an attempt to fashion a philosophical glossary that would remove some of the ambiguities traditionally associated with linguistic usage in philosophy. For example, take the term 'relation.' It is generally used to apply indifferently to connections among things and connections among words. Dewey and Bentley, as I recall, propose that the term 'relation' should be restricted just to connections among words, while the term 'connections' should be used for relationships among things. I think their distinction has merit, but I would use 'connections' and 'relationships' interchangeably to refer to connections that things have with one another."

"But why do you introduce the distinction at this particular point?"

"Because both Piaget and Vygotsky talk about the internalization of social relationships, and I simply want to distinguish the 'external' social *relationships* from the 'internal' logical and linguistic *relations*. Relations may be thought of as internalized relationships, and relationships may be considered externalized relations."

Natasha stops her note-taking and looks at me in that very direct way many European women have. (I don't mean *bold*; I mean something closer to *straightforward and frank*.) "Would you please do me a favor? Would you try to cite references wherever possible? Like that work by Dewey and Bentley; what was it called?"

"*Knowing and the Known.*" I add, "Published, I think, in 1949."

"*Knowing and the Known,*" she repeats, as she writes it down. "1949."

"Look," I say, "I can't always remember what the sources are, and even when I can, it's incredibly pedantic to cite them in the middle of a conversation. I'll tell you what I'll do: I'll go over the manuscripts later and pencil in the sources I recall, okay?"

She gives me a conciliatory glance and nods agreement. There follows a long, audible sigh whose meaning I cannot surmise. She gets up, strolls around my office, and studies the books in my bookcases. Then she sits down again. "Let's go."

I fail to respond because my thoughts are elsewhere. Natasha is becoming increasingly enigmatic to me. I find her intriguing, but the purpose of *my* inquiry is not to understand *her*. Besides, she raises some interesting philosophical questions. Philosophers are always puzzling over the reality of fictional characters: Is Huck Finn real or isn't he? But what about the fictionality of real characters? There are times when Natasha seems to me more fiction than fact. But to tell the truth, there are times when I seem equally that way to myself.

There's a slight edge of impatience in her voice this time: "Can we go on?"

"Where were we?"

"You had said, in I.5 of your outline, that human relationships can be portrayed in such a way as to be analyzable into logical relations. What do you have in mind when you say this — Piaget, Vygotsky, or something else?"

"All three. First, Piaget. It seems to me that both Piaget and Vygotsky assert that there is a process of 'interiorization,' as Piaget calls it, or 'internalization,' as Vygotsky calls it. But Piaget sees it as developing more toward the middle of childhood, as the result of the suppression of egocentrism in the child, while Vygotsky contends that it happens much earlier, as external dialogue is transformed into inner speech, and inner speech leads to thinking. So this is where the hard claims of Piaget's stage theory come into conflict with the more fluid analysis by Vygotsky. On the other hand, Piaget seems to me very acute and perceptive when he alludes to the derivation of logical relations from social relationships. This is to be found in any number of his books, such as the last pages of *The Grasp of Consciousness*. There's a very nice statement of his position cited here in Barbara Rogoff's *Apprenticeship in Thinking*." I brandish the book at Natasha for a moment, then turn to page 145 and read aloud:

> Piaget suggests that cooperation provides an impetus to order thought in logical operations that involve a system of propositions that are free from contradiction and are reversible: "Thinking in common promotes non-contradiction: It is much easier to contradict oneself, when one thinks for oneself (egocentrism) than when some partners are there to remember what one has said before and the propositions that one has agreed to admit."

The source that Rogoff cites is Piaget's 1977 work, *Les Operations logiques et la vie sociale*. For Piaget, then, social cooperation in discourse leads to the coordination of perspective or points of view, and this leads in turn to the coordination of propositions, involving logical consistency as well as other logical operations.

Natasha takes all of this in and ponders it, leaning back in her chair, her chin in her hand, her finger against her cheek. I am at the point of associating the posture with that of a therapist when I am interrupted by a pang of bad conscience. She has done nothing to deserve such a condescending categorization from me, and I should keep my thoughts on my work and keep them, in any event, to myself. Even so, another small voice reminds me to follow the inquiry wherever it leads, so that I find myself hung up on an internal self-contradiction.

"Can you give me another example of the derivation of logical relations from human relationships?" Natasha asks.

"Social life is full of reciprocity, obviously. I speak and you listen; then you speak and I listen. I open the door for you, then you open the next door for me. I reach out to shake your hand; you reach out to shake mine. I insult you; you insult me. Social life is a web of such reciprocal behaviors, ranging from cooperation to vengeance. When we remove the behavioral or cultural husks, we are left with the logical kernel — the abstract understanding of reversibility. If New York is far from Moscow, then Moscow is far from New York. If you are as tall as I am, then I am as tall as you are. Thus reciprocity in social behavior translates into symmetry in logical relations. With symmetrical relations, if the first formulation is true, then the reverse formulation *must* also be true."

"What about nonreversibility?"

"There are plenty of examples of that, too. I can think of one in the conversation we were having earlier, while we were standing on that little knoll and looking at the skyline of Manhattan. You remarked, as I recall, 'Your inquiry is the subject of my inquiry, but mine is not the subject of yours.' But we have to distinguish cases in which (1) the reverse necessarily follows from cases (2) in which the reverse necessarily does *not* follow and from cases (3) in which it is undetermined whether the reverse follows or doesn't follow. Thus, if it is true that I am taller than you, then it is necessarily false that you are taller than me. On the other hand, if it is true that Ivan is kicking Pyotr, nothing follows as to whether or not Pyotr is kicking Ivan."

"And if Sam likes Lucy, it is indeterminate whether or not Lucy likes Sam."

"Right."

"So the logic of relations is an internalization of one aspect of social relationships."

"So it seems to me, and evidently so it seemed to Piaget and Vygotsky."

"Therefore, you are arguing, if we *portray* children engaged in social processes that display reciprocity, transitivity, symmetry, and the like, then we will be providing them with a model that they can emulate. They then engage in similar processes in the classroom, and when they do, they tend to internalize the logical aspects of those processes in the form of a logic of relations."

"Of course," I reply. "But we constantly get muddled with regard to these distinctions. If we get hit, we think we absolutely have to hit back. Or if we borrow money, we may think of all sorts of pretexts for not repaying it. And I needn't tell you how wild our inferences are when it comes to indeterminate cases. The confusions about what can be legitimately inferred and what cannot be are often extremely mischievous. This is why the portrait of children making these distinctions clearly should result in better reasoning among the children who internalize that portrait."

"Is that why you began your first novel, *Harry Stottlemeier's Discovery*, with Harry confusing a reversible statement and a nonreversible statement?"

"Yes, although strictly speaking, reversibility and convertibility are not quite the same thing. Convertibility, which is the subject of Chapter 1 of *Harry*, is a special case of reversibility."

"I don't understand."

"Certain relationships are symmetrical, like 'is far from' and 'is equal to' and 'is worth as much as.' So if it is true that four quarters are worth as much as a dollar, then it is also true that a dollar is worth as much as four quarters. But the first chapter in *Harry* deals with the notion of convertibility, as derived from the classical logic of Plato and Aristotle. In that logic, statements begin with 'all,' 'some,' and 'no.' Some of these stay true when the subject-term and the predicate-term are exchanged, and some become false. If it is true that no pancakes are geese, then it must be true that no geese are pancakes. If it is true that some children are thoughtful people, then it must be true that some thoughtful people are children. On the other hand, if it is true, as Socrates says in the *Euthyphro*, that all evens are numbers, it doesn't follow that all numbers are evens."

"So the logic you have in your program for children teaches them the right way to draw inferences?"

"Perhaps it would be better to say that it shows them some of the unreliable ways they would do well to avoid."

Natasha studies the piece of calligraphy on the wall of my office, with its seven different versions of the Chinese word for *thinking*. "Still," she says pensively, "your approach in philosophy is different from ours in psychology. You are normative; we're descriptive. We talk about how people do in fact think and you talk about how they ought to think."

I shrug. "You draw normative inferences from your descriptions of how thinking takes place in fact, while our prescriptions about how thinking ought to occur are usually based on our assumptions about how it does happen in fact. So we're not necessarily that far apart, but the educators who rely on us complain that they keep getting mixed messages from us."

"I'm not surprised," she murmurs. Then she straightens up and says, more briskly. "I must get the bus back to New York. I'll call you." In an instant, she's gone.

SECOND VISIT

We were to meet the following Friday, and presumably for a series of Fridays thereafter, but Thursday afternoon Natasha called to say she evidently had a touch of flu. The following week the flu was still hanging on, and she seemed, in our brief phone conversation, to be somewhat depressed.

The week after that she does show up, looking, I think, a bit pale, but otherwise all right. She has hardly had a few sips of coffee than she pounces on me, "How did you think it went, the last time?"

"Our reciprocal inquiry? I thought it went fine. Didn't you?"

She shakes her head vigorously. "I thought it started out all right, but by the end it was terrible!"

I am astonished, and ask her why she thinks it was so bad.

"Because," she says tensely, "after a while you stop inquiring and begin lecturing. Whenever I ask a question, you have a standard answer all ready. It's like listening to a tape recorder!"

I stare at her so unbelievingly that she is unable to conceal her amusement. Rightly or wrongly, I interpret this as a bit of a taunt and I feel somewhat annoyed. "Look, Natasha—" I begin to say in a prim, avuncular fashion, "if I have the answers to your questions, why shouldn't I give them to you? Why should I beat around the bush? I detest those cat-and-mouse games that teachers play with students! Granted, I don't know much, but what I know I should be able to tell you, if it's just some pieces of information that you're lacking."

As I go on in this manner, I become increasingly uncomfortable. Finally I say, "Natasha, this is ridiculous. As I think over what I was just saying, I'm reminded of Descartes, in his egregious conceit, remarking that he may not have divine omniscience, but what little he knows, he knows as well as God does."

"Didn't one of your American philosophers, Peirce, say 'There is only one commandment: Do not block the road to inquiry'?"

"Something like that," I agree. "I usually admonish teachers, 'Be philosophically self-effacing! Don't lecture kids! Let them find out for themselves and in the process learn to think for themselves!'"

Natasha looks more relaxed now, and her voice, as she speaks, seems to have acquired a faint purr. "I overreacted, and I'm sorry," she says gently. "But you know, I've been dipping into Dewey, and he says somewhere that the schools make the mistake of substituting the refined end-products of inquiry for the gross, raw subject-matter of inquiry. So what I thought you were doing — wasn't that an example of what Dewey was objecting to?"

I nod agreement: "Dewey sees it as one of the major errors of our civilization. What happens in the experiment becomes codified in the textbook, and then the textbook replaces the experiment in the schools. Education becomes didactic instead of remaining experimental. Children must be taught to inquire for themselves and not simply learn by heart the results of the inquiries of others."

Natasha rummages among her notes and comes up with, "'If we want to inspire children to emulate greatness, it would seem that we must try to arrange for them to study the great cultural products of the critical, imaginative and scientific spirit — the scientific and humanistic achievements of mankind — under conditions resembling as much as possible those in which such achievements were created.' You yourself said that, in the Preface to *Growing Up with Philosophy*" (Lipman and Sharp, 1978, p. x).

"Now who's being scholarly?" I ask.

One eyebrow arches slightly. "I'm leading up to something. There is, in Davydov, an emphasis on knowledge through reenactment — am I not right?"

"Yes, of course. It's an emphasis that goes back to Vico, at least. To understand something — say, a pair of shoes — requires the reenactment of the making of those shoes, according to Vico and subsequent thinkers."

"Is that true only of artifacts, or is it true of natural objects as well?"

"I didn't say I thought it was true, because if it were true at all, I think it could be only partially true. But as for your question, there's nothing to prevent us from trying to understand things in terms of their natural development. The best example I know is the effort by Paul Valéry to understand a seashell by trying to understand how it came into being. And, of course, Davydov talks about all of this as 'the embryology of truth'."

Natasha toys with the metal sculpture of an owl that normally keeps watch over the table. "Peru?" she asks.

"Close enough," I say. "Chile."

We sip our coffees in silence. I have a feeling we have reached some kind of turning point. Finally, Natasha says, "You mention Davydov. What are we going to do about him?"

"What would you like to do about him?"

"Well, you've been reading his *Problems of Developmental Teaching* in the English version, and I'm already familiar with the Russian version. Why don't we talk about Davydov? Not in general, of course, but how you see his thinking meshing with our own? It would be an area where your familiarity would not outweigh mine so much, and you might be less — less — "

"Didactic?"

"Thanks. Didactic."

"Have you looked at the English translation? It appeared in three sequential issues of *Soviet Education* in 1988, under a variety of different titles" (1988a, 1988b, 1988c, 1988d, 1988e).

Soviet Education published only the first two and the last two chapters. The remainder, Chapters 3 and 4, were considered too theoretical, so they were transferred to *Soviet Psychology* and may be published eventually in that periodical. She tells me that she has read the *Soviet Education* chapters and has made notes on them. She implies that the translation is far from adequate.

"That's what I thought, too," I agree. "Well, why don't we go back to my reference a bit earlier to Davydov's phrase, 'the embryology of truth'?"

"It wasn't Davydov's phrase," Natasha corrects me. "It was Skatkin's."

"Oh? Well, but Davydov apparently admires Skatkin's work very much — " (1988c).

" — and quite rightly!"

I pause momentarily to try to understand the reasons for Natasha's vehemence but fail utterly, so I go on, "Look, when we come across a particular topic, like learning through reenactment, would it be too, too didactic a procedure to share our notes with one another?"

Natasha ignores my attempt at irony and says soberly but softly, "All I ask is that we work cooperatively and with mutual respect. Since our individual objectives are different, we have nothing to compete about. And since we share the same subject-matter — Vygotsky, Davydov, Dewey, your stuff for children — we will both benefit by finding out in what ways our disclosures of that subject-matter are similar and in what ways they are different."

I put my head back on the edge of my high-backed chair and stare at the ceiling. "Good! I like the way you've put it. But I would still like to concentrate on Davydov, at least to begin with — if that's all right with you."

"Of course it's all right with me. Let's go back to the notions of knowledge through reenactment and the embryology of truth."

"Yes, well, this is where Davydov pays homage to Hegel (1988b). Hegel draws a double analogy: between the way the consciousness of the individual develops and the way the consciousness of humankind develops. And then he suggests, in *The Phenomenology of Mind*, that the world itself moves from a mute, inanimate status to consciousness and then on to self-consciousness in a manner similar to the development that occurs in humans."

Natasha looks at me suspiciously. "But Davydov isn't an advocate of the recapitulation theory in the strict or literal sense. What he says is that, as children learn, they execute mental actions commensurate with actions whereby these products of spiritual culture have been historically elicited (1988c). The key word is 'commensurate': between these different processes, he sees some kind of proportionality, that's all" (1988a).

Warming to the topic, I hasten to agree: "Yes, right. Davydov cites Hegel on this point, but he could just as well cite Leibniz, when he (Davydov) says that every nuance of human development, such as a thumbnail sketch or a children's game, is representative of the essence of human development. Davydov recognizes here how important this is for pedagogy: by means of curriculum exercises that are representative of the discipline from which they are derived, we can teach children how to master their cognitive processes. At the same time, there is compressed in each of our pedagogical successes, the entire history of education" (1988b).

"I'd like to come back to Skatkin," Natasha says, a faint unsteadiness in her voice. "In the 1970s and early 1980s, I was naturally an avid student of his books, such as *The Improvement of the Teaching Process*, published in 1971, and *Some Problems of Modern Didactics*, which he edited in 1982. But I also knew him personally and I thought the world of him. You can see how sound and practical he was just by those passages of his that Davydov cites, such as that it is essential for children who are assimilating a new technique of action to become acquainted 'with those questions that were asked by the person who was the first to resolve similar tasks'" (in Davydov, 1988c, p. 39).

"I agree," I say. "It's an impressive form of peer modeling and of reenactment of the steps leading up to a discovery."

"That's it!" Natasha exclaims, quite animated now. "Skatkin speaks of a 'problem-based exposition of knowledge' in which 'the teacher not only communicates final scientific conclusions to the children but in some measure also reproduces the path whereby those conclusions are reached.' This is what is meant by the phrase 'the embryology of truth.' In so doing, Skatkin goes on to say (following Davydov's quotation of him), that the teacher *demonstrates to the pupils the very route taken by scientific thought,* obliges the pupils *to trace the dialectical movement of thought* toward the truth, and makes them, as it were, co-participants in scientific exploration'" (in Davydov, 1988c, p. 16).

"Does that describe our collaboration, too?" I ask. "I focus on certain sets of conclusions and you focus on the path by which they were arrived at? And are these two things similar to the two that are involved in 'complex thinking'—the substantive and the procedural aspects of a given inquiry?"

"I suspect so," Natasha replies. "Can we take a break?" Ungenerously I wonder just how taken with Skatkin she actually was.

"I was beginning to feel claustrophobic again," Natasha confides. "Have you any remedies for that?"

We are strapping on the safety belts in my Festiva. I have suggested a ride around the college vicinity. But then I take her reference to claustrophobia a bit more seriously and proceed toward Garret Mountain.

"Garret Mountain," I explain, not knowing whether I'm being tedious or not, "is to the long ridge of First Mountain as the dot of an exclamation point is to the exclamation point." It's really nothing much more than a hill, but it gives quite a view of the sprawling urban expanse that this portion of northern New Jersey has become.

We sit in the car at the lookout point, deterred by the icy wind from standing by the parapet. Natasha is absorbed in writing in her notepad. She writes very quickly, but whether in Russian or in English I do not know. "You remind me of Nabokov," I venture. "I understand he wrote and even thought equally well in Russian and in English."

She continues her rapid scribbling, saying only "Hmmm." Then with a little flourish she finishes and slaps the notepad closed. She seems satisfied and somewhat amused. "You want to talk about translation." Half question, half assertion.

"No," I protest. "We were discussing Davydov. Let's go on with him."

Now she grins. "We don't have to be fetishistic about it. We can go wherever the inquiry takes us, even though there are many leads, and even though some don't seem to connect very well at first with others. As in a classroom dialogue, there are many lines of reasoning at first, and it is only gradually that they begin to converge."

"That's the difference between a vertical theological and a horizontal naturalistic consciousness," I remark. "The one, as in Eudora Welty, claims that 'all that rises must converge.' The other claims that 'all that inquires must converge'."

"Perhaps," she concedes. "In any case, you've written somewhere that translation is an important manner of thinking, and I've been meaning to ask you why you said that."

I had turned the car engine off when we arrived, but now I start it up again so that the heater can keep us from becoming icicles. "Well, all right," I concede, "I won't try to connect it directly with what we were talking about in the case of Davydov. Nevertheless I think that what Vygotsky and Piaget and Davydov and Dewey would all agree to is, as I just said, that the schools should convert children into inquirers."

"Wouldn't it be better to say that the schools should try to preserve and develop the natural propensity for inquiry that children bring with them?"

"That's what I should have said, of course," I acknowledge. "But this 'propensity for inquiry,' as you call it, involves both competencies and skills. Students may have a particular skill — say, that of formulating questions — but they may lack the competency to employ that skill in suitable circumstances."

Natasha nods. "Right. And even if they have both the requisite competencies and skills, they may fail to employ them because we have failed to motivate them to do so by neglecting to provide them with suitable incentives."

"Well, okay," I continue. "But let's put aside for the time being these questions of competencies, motivations, and incentives, and let's focus on the skills. I mean the skills essential to doing inquiry in a school setting, not skills in general. This has led me to talk about four kinds of thinking skills. First are those involved in investigating or examining a problematic subject-matter. They range from formulating hypotheses to gathering and sifting evidence, from designing experiments to testing predictions. Second are reasoning skills, which have to do not with the acquisition of knowledge but with its coordination, extension, and defense. Third are concept-formation skills, which involve the organizing of diffuse information into manageable clusters. And fourth are the translation skills, which we started to talk about a few minutes ago."

"You call the first kind 'inquiry skills'?"

"For lack of a better name. They are the skills employed in doing science."

"And how would you characterize translation skills? What do they enable us to do?"

"They enable us to keep meanings intact despite changes of context. For example, when you translate a sentence from Russian to English, your primary objective is to preserve the original meaning it had in Russian and restate it so that it has the same meaning in English. But any such shift from one symbolic scheme to another, for example, from an algebraic formula to a graph, or from time as expressed by a sundial to time expressed digitally — all of these are meaning-preservative operations and require translation skills."

"So translation enables us to preserve meanings from context to context, and reasoning enables us to preserve truth, through the course of an argument, from premises to conclusion."

"Right. It might be useful to note here that psychologists use the terms 'fluency' and 'flexibility' for somewhat similar purposes, with regard to translation. I mean, if you speak Russian well, you are 'fluent' in Russian. But if you speak both Russian and English well, and are fluent in both, you have 'flexibility.' There are countless modes of human expression, ranging from music to mathematics, and all can be involved in fluency or flexibility or both."

"What would you say all this about translation has to do with what we were talking about before?" Before I can answer, Natasha adds, "What's the connection between translation skills and the transition from dialogue to thinking, or the understanding of a thing through reenacting how it came to be, or the way an individual's growth recapitulates the growth of its species?"

"That's a tough one," I answer. "But I think each of the cases you cite involves some kind of preservation, and it is debatable, to say the least, whether the characteristics allegedly preserved have remained intact and identical with the original, or whether they have been so modified by the transition as to be substantively different. And by the way, I'm aware of what you're doing by asking me to connect what we've just discussed with what we talked about earlier."

She grins. "Are you now?"

"Yes, because connecting is thinking. When E. M. Forster said, 'Only connect,' that's what he meant: only think."

Natasha makes no comment, but gets out of the car and begins walking along the parapet to the path that runs precariously close to the face of the cliff. Of course to me, any proximity to a sheer drop is perilous, and I am instantly alarmed. "Hey, come back here, that's dangerous!" I call out. But I might as well try to deter a mountain goat, and she picks her way nimbly over ledges and around boulders. At length she returns, her face flushed and animated, her eyes glistening. By the amused way she looks at me, I suspect I must be a bit paler than usual.

We drive back to the Institute with hardly a word between us. Natasha sands a fingernail broken on a boulder and hums softly to herself. For a moment I wonder if I feel a bit depressed *because* she's in such a good humor, but it's a thought I promptly put out of my mind.

*   *   *   *

As I ready a fresh pot of coffee in the kitchen of the Institute, I reflect upon the incident and conclude that what I am feeling is the kind of resentment one often experiences with the clinical ministrations of a therapist or "shrink." I think Natasha's audacity frightened me in more ways than one, and I begin to wonder if her true objective is limited to an examination of the methodological aspect of our inquiry. It even occurs to me that she might be one of those people, like espionage agents, who feel fully alive only in an atmosphere of intense danger.

Fortunately, these intimations evaporate as our conversation recommences and she asks, "How did you discover Vygotsky?"

"Funny you should ask," I say. "Only yesterday I saw Ann Paul's film, *The Butterflies of Zagorsk*, which is about Vygotsky's work with deaf–blind children. It's very moving."

"You saw it at home, on television?"

"No, we don't have a TV set. I played a copy on the VCR here on campus."

Her tone clinical again, Natasha repeats her question, "So how did you discover Vygotsky?"

"I asked myself that question just recently, and pretty soon I began to think my memory was playing tricks on me. My recollection was that I had read Vygotsky's first book in English, *Thought and Language*, in the late 1940s. But when I checked the publication date, it was 1962. The discrepancy puzzled me: how could I be so far off? Then I noticed a translator's remark that solved everything. In 1939, *Psychiatry* had published the final chapter of *Thought and Language*, and it must have been that article with which I was so familiar. I was sure of this because I could remember the long afternoons I would spend in Columbia University's psychology library, while I was a graduate student, going through back issues of the psychology journals. I especially recalled going through the back issues of *Psychiatry* and finding Vygotsky's article there."

"You published your first article in *Psychiatry* also, didn't you?"

"It was one of the first. It came out in 1956. It had to do with the sociopathology of charisma. It was a theme that, I take it, also interested Vygotsky. So I infer, at any rate, from James Wertsch's discussion in his *Vygotsky and the Social Formation of Mind*" (pp. 217–223).

"Can you trace any connections between what Vygotsky had to say in that final chapter and your curriculum for philosophy in the elementary school?"

"There are certainly similarities, but I'm not sure that there are direct causal connections. I was reading all sorts of things at that time, especially the phenomenological stuff, that made the same point and that would have reinforced what Vygotsky had to say."

"But is there a pattern of one-to-one correlations between Vygotskian concepts and curriculum episodes?"

"Yes, I think so, although I haven't done a study to show that that's the case. But look, let me take a particular example. There's a passage in the novel, *Suki*, that I'd like you to read first." I hand her the book, open to page 17, and ask her to read from line 26 on that page to line 26 on page 19:

Suki looked at him soberly. "Harry, right now, tell me, what's going on?"

He looked at her wonderingly. "Around us?"

"If you like."

Harry grimaced and squinted upwards. "The sun is shining," he said finally.

"Anything else?"

He concentrated, then announced, "The stream is flowing."

Suki's face lighted up, and she said gently, "Okay, fine, that's a beginning."

He was mystified. "A beginning? A beginning to what?"

"Never mind," Suki countered, "Let's just talk about those two sentences."

"The sun is shining and the stream is flowing? What's there to talk about? That's all there is to say about them!"

"Well, I could ask you if they're true."

"Of course they're true!" Harry exclaimed vehemently.

"The sun shines?"

"Yup!"

"And the stream flows?"

"Yup!"

"Would it be possible for the sun not to shine?"

"Sure, but then it wouldn't any longer be a sun."

"And would it be possible for the stream not to flow?"

"Yes, but then it wouldn't be a stream."

"So when I asked you what's going on, you didn't really think about what was actually happening; you just told me what suns always do and what streams always do."

Harry looked at his hands. "I told you I can't write. And see, it's because I can't think of anything to say — except what's obvious!"

But Suki had no intention of allowing him to feel sorry for himself.

"Harry," she said.

"What?"

"Look up at the sky with your eyes almost closed. That's right, squint. Do you still see the sun?"

"No."

"What do you see?"

"I see — I see — a shining."

"And now look down — over there, what do you see?"

Harry squinted at Belcher's Brook. "I see something moving."

"Moving?"

"Well, flowing — or running, maybe."

"So you see a flowing?"

He nodded, still perplexed.

"Harry, I'm just trying to get you to pay closer attention and to be more accurate when you say what happens. What I'm getting at is, first you see a shining, right, and then you say it's the sun. Or first you see a flowing, and then you say it's the stream. So wouldn't it be more accurate to say, 'There's a shining that is the sun,' or 'There's a flowing that is stream'?"

He stared at her, then managed to say, "You mean, turn the sentences around?"

"Why not — if it's a better way of saying how things happen!"

"But we don't talk that way! We couldn't —"

"Maybe we couldn't, maybe we could," Suki interrupted. "But still, we can write that way, can't we?"

Harry looked dubious. "Sure, I suppose we can. But why bother?"

"Well, if I were writing a poem, I wouldn't say, 'The sun is shining' unless I wanted something very flat and matter-of-fact at that point. I'd more likely say, 'Shining is the sun' — I'd turn it around because that's more like the way it happens."

"So first we're aware of a flowing, and then later we call what's flowing a river or a stream?"

"Right."

"And there's no such thing as a river that doesn't flow?"

"Right."

"Well, then, maybe our language is all mixed up. We use nouns where there should be verbs, and verbs where there should be nouns. If you're right, we shouldn't say, 'The river is flowing.' We should say, 'The flow is rivering.'"

Suki laughed again. Harry thought it resembled the tinkle of the glass wind chimes Millie had brought to school last year. "Or, 'The shine is sunning' instead of 'The sun is shining.'"

"Now," I continue, "in the final chapter of the first Vygotsky book, he elaborates on the notion that our 'inner speech' consists largely of predication. That is, it concentrates on the predicates of statements, with the result that inner speech is highly telescoped and intense, being largely composed of adjectives and adverbs, like 'shining' and 'flowing' and 'quickly.' It is only when we are forced into more formal types of expression, such as written speech, that we place the abstract subject-terms at the beginning of our sentences, even though they are largely conceptual rather than experiential."

"From many experiences of a shining in the sky, we develop the concept of the sun, and we proceed to the inference that shining is a property of the sun," Natasha murmurs.

"Right," I agree. "Of course, twentieth-century philosophy has devoted itself very often to blasting the classical metaphysics according to which the world is made up of things having properties or of substances having attributes. I'm thinking especially of Dewey, Whitehead, Heidegger, and Buchler. But let me not get started on this: It leads off in too many different directions."

"So what are you telling me? Are the incidents in the novels translations of particular aspects of psychological theories — or philosophical theories — or aren't they?" Natasha demands, visibly puzzled.

All I can reply is, "Each episode has its own history — its own story. In some cases the theories precede the illustrations, and in other cases the illustrations precede the theories. I'm sorry to complicate your aspect of our inquiry this way, but there is no single, simple methodology here."

I realize, on saying this, that it sounds a bit irritable. At the same time, I am aware that Natasha means to be provocative. Her job, as she understands it, is to intervene in whatever ways are needed to get me to produce and display the methodology I rely on in engaging in my own sorts of inquiry. Like a Vygotskian teacher, for whom "teaching precedes development and draws it up behind," her queries are intended to draw me out. My own reaction is that of the oyster, which, when anyone tries to pry its shells apart, clamps them together ever more tightly. Except that I have now begun to wonder if such a panic reaction is any longer necessary — if it ever was.

With these thoughts circling about like buzzards in my mind, I tell her "See you next week!" and watch her walk jauntily off in the direction of the bus stop.

THIRD VISIT

Natasha arrives just as the first snowflakes of the winter begin to fall. Silently, we watch them scatter across the grass that is visible from my office.

Eventually, I say, "Would it be all right with you if we were to devote the first portion of each session to Davydov? Otherwise, I'm afraid we'll not deal with him as extensively as I'd like."

She shrugs. "Why not? Surely you have an agenda?"

"I have some subject-areas picked out — some are much more complex or more closely examined by Davydov than others — but I haven't arranged them in any sequence as yet. They are:

Action and activity
Teaching and development
Internalization, appropriation, and reenactment
Consciousness and reflection
The priority of the abstract
Problem-solving

Of these, the last two I've listed are the most detailed. For example, under "problem-solving," I've listed the subheadings of modeling, mediation, practice, planning, monitoring, evaluation, research, and formative experiments."

"And have you a suggestion for what we are to take up during the remainder of each session?"

"We can do as we like," I answer. "We can discuss Vygotsky or Mead or Philosophy for Children — whatever. What do you think?"

"Whenever I hear the word 'agenda,' I instinctively shiver," she responds. Then she sighs and adds resignedly, "But if that's the only way you can operate, I guess I can manage to go along with it."

"Why the hesitation?"

"Because," she says sharply, "what's important is not these people in isolation, but the connections we can discover among them. We have to compare and contrast them, find out what they have in common and what gulfs separate them."

"Agreed," I say. "All that needs to be done, and we can do it. But I still think we have to concentrate on Davydov because his position has been formulated most recently and is least well known."

"Just don't lecture me. I warn you: I'll pass out!"

"I seldom make promises."

"Are you confessing to being spiritually stingy?"

I let it pass. Natasha's obviously in a feisty mood today. I merely inquire, "So where should we begin?"

"Why not with 'teaching and development'? It's what links Davydov most closely with traditional Vygotskyan theory."

"You think he deviates in some ways from Vygotsky?"

"Not with regard to teaching and development."

"Okay," I say. "We agree. What Davydov calls 'developmental teaching' is a unity rather than two separate things, the way some psychologists have assumed (1988b). Just as you can't make sweeping statements about an organism without taking its environment into account, so you can't make sweeping statements about children's minds without taking the history of their encounter with their social environment into account. And the chief factors in that history are the form of their family upbringing and the form of their teacher's interventions" (1988e).

"So Davydov sees the opposition between Vygotsky and Piaget as being a very sharp one?"

"Yes, as Davydov and Vygotsky understand Piaget, he is saying that 'the indicator of the level of a child's thought is not what the child knows, nor what he is capable of learning, but how he thinks in an area where he has no knowledge at all' (Davydov, 1988b, p. 50). This means that, for Piaget, 'teaching should orient itself towards the mature things that the child can do on her own' (ibid.). But this is to take the line of least resistance (ibid., p. 51). The criterion should not be what the child can understand immediately and on her own, but what the child, if given assistance now, will be able to do tomorrow (ibid.). The aim must be to bring children — *all* children — to maturity" (ibid.).

Natasha remarks, "So Davydov subscribes — as you do, too, presumably — to Vygotsky's zone of proximal development."

"Of course. I agree with them that teaching calls to life a whole series of developmental processes that it would not otherwise be possible to elicit in the child. But, of course, it has to be teaching of the right sort, and here I don't think Davydov tells us enough. Oh, he does say things I obviously subscribe to, such as that teachers should 'shape in children the skill of identifying objects and their parts and, above all, the relationships between them' (1988e, p. 5). On the other hand, I am not so sure that the teacher should strive to guess where each child is headed and direct the child's actions toward the embodiment of what the child has in mind. It sounds good, but it may demand too much of the teacher."

"You would agree, nonetheless, that the zone of proximal development is that aspect of Vygotsky that non-Soviet psychologists have most widely acclaimed."

"Certainly," I reply. "First, because it corrects a weakness in the Piagetian approach and second, because it lends itself so readily to implementation and experimentation."

"Have you always been critical of Piaget on this point?"

"Well, yes and no," I tell her. "When I was teaching Piaget at Columbia College in the 1960s, I was strongly in favor of his position, as I understood it. In fact, when I later aimed *Harry* at 11- and 12-year-olds, it was with the understanding that that would be the period—the beginning of the formal stage, as he called it—at which they could begin to deal effectively with the formal logic that I had put in *Harry*. It was my thought, when I wrote *Harry*, that children would be able to read it and enjoy it without adult assistance. It was only over the next four or five years that my views began to change, and I began to admit that they would need help from parents and teachers. So I wasn't always an advocate of the zone of proximal development."

Natasha suppresses a yawn and stretches. "Can we go out for a while? It's a beautiful day!"

"You promise you won't scare me again by playing mountain goat?"

She laughs. "I'll promise no such thing. I'm a trained mountain climber."

"Hmmm. I would have thought it more likely you were a trained cave explorer."

Natasha doesn't respond to my heavy-handed irony. I am reminded of my own counsel to teachers to avoid irony in dealing with children. It is a weapon they either can't use or won't use, and it escalates so quickly that it's out of hand before you know it. I have it on the tip of my tongue to say to her, apologetically, that I was only trying to be humorous, but I figure the less said about it the better.

We decamp to the parking lot, alongside the Institute, without further conversation.

*   *   *   *

"Where are we going?" Natasha asks, as we head north by car on Valley Road. "This is the same way we went last week."

"But last week we went to West Paterson. Today we're going to Paterson."

"What's in Paterson?"

It is on the tip of my tongue to say, "You'll see," but I check myself at the last moment and instead say, "The Great Falls."

She laughs. "Great? How great?"

"Second largest in the East, after Niagara Falls."

She looks eager and expectant as we approach the Great Falls and she can hear the roar of the cataract as it tumbles into the gorge. "I had no idea you had such impressive landscape in the vicinity of the college!" she exclaims. She explores the narrow metal bridge that spans the rocky channel and the turbulent water far below. Her face is radiant. "I love water—oceans, lakes, rivers, waterfalls! I love it in every form it takes!"

"You're gushing!" I observe.

"You're so perceptive!" she returns. Then she adds, "Please. I'm enjoying this. Let me be."

She watches the water cascade down and the clouds of mist rising in the crisp winter air and glistening in the sun. Ten minutes go by. I'm beginning to feel cold. Twenty minutes go by; I'm chilled through. Finally, she turns to me and says, "Let's go!"

We head toward the car parked on one of the side streets. I can't wait to get the heater going.

A roadside diner is too much to pass up and we stop for coffee. It's all chrome, glitz, and overstuffed furniture covered in black Naugahyde. But the waitress is quick and pleasant, and the coffee isn't bad.

Natasha purses her lips in a way that signals the advent of a question about which she has been thinking for some time. Finally, she says, "You were saying earlier that you endorsed the theory of the zone of proximal development. But your actual practice doesn't accord with the theory."

"How's that?"

"The theory stipulates *adult* mediation between the culture and the child, whether in the case of parental upbringing or of classroom teachers providing instruction. In your practice, it seems to me, the role of the teacher is somewhat downgraded, and more reliance is placed on the text and on the student's peers. I mean, look at the two-page outline you gave me: You ascribe to the text precisely the mediating functions—both culturally and historically—that Vygotsky and Davydov ascribe to the teacher."

"I agree: This is an important discrepancy between my approach and theirs. But the question of what role the text is to play in education is hardly a new one: It stretches back to the pedagogical role Plato expected his dialogues to play and the opposition to that role that was generated in the years after Plato's demise."

Natasha drains her cup of its remaining coffee and observes, "But the case is just the opposite when it comes to the child's peers, isn't that so?"

"Yes, elementary school philosophy stresses the building of a classroom community of inquiry in which children can learn from one another as well as from the teacher and the text. In the case of skill-acquisition — as opposed to content-acquisition — this learning from one's peers is particularly important. We're only just beginning to understand the significance of friendships in school settings and of sibling relationships in the home. Earlier in this century, partly due to Freud's influence, most of the emphasis was on parent–child or teacher–child relationships. The development of social solidarity among children in the classroom was actively discouraged. Do you agree?"

She shrugs mischievously. "What difference would it make to you whether I agreed or not?"

The young woman behind the cash register has kind eyes, wears very heavy makeup, and speaks with an accent. She and Natasha chat for a few moments while I wait in the tiny outside foyer.

Natasha settles back into her chair in my office, presses the tips of her fingers together, and says slowly, "In part I, item 4 of your outline, you speak of the text as a 'peculiar object of perception that carries mental reflection already within itself.' This is Davydov's phrase, isn't it?"

"Yes, he uses it somewhere. I suppose that what he has in mind is to distinguish natural objects like stones and trees, from which all reflection is absent, from artifacts like automobiles and books. But these artifacts themselves fall into two groups, because both are the products of deliberate human making and carry the intelligence of their makers in the form of the intelligence of their designs. Books, however, are not only thoughtful in their design: They carry thought within themselves, as mothers do unborn children."

"And so the merit of this last category . . . "

I interrupt. "Its merit is that it serves admirably as a springboard for discussion, and discussion, in turn, is the generative matrix of student thinking. Look, I can use an analogy with the refining of ores. Low-grade ores need high-grade refining equipment; high-grade ores can be refined using only low-grade equipment. The same is true of stimuli to discussion. Those who are moved to discuss natural objects are generally experts — like paleontologists discussing rock strata. But books contain ready-made ideas and ready-made contrasts among ideas, so that they are ideal for sparking discussions, even among young readers who bring little specialized experience to bear upon their reading."

Natasha scowls a bit and remarks, "Are you making a case for the intrinsic superiority—when it comes to educating for thinking—of education in the humanities over science education?"

"No, I'm only contrasting certain preliminary considerations. The science educator can overcome the handicap of the fact that quarks contain no reflection within themselves by concentrating on the thinking that went into the discovery of the quark. One of the most exciting courses I took when I was a student at Columbia was Lloyd Motz's course on astronomy, in which he showed the theoretical problems posed by each successive twentieth-century physicist—Bohr, Dirac, Schrödinger, and so on—and how they then went about trying to solve those problems."

Natasha pauses in her furious note-taking and turns to a fresh page in her notebook. "Let's go back," she says, "to the role of the text and what you say about it in the first three subheadings of your outline. You speak of it there as (1) a model of a community of inquiry; (2) a reflection of the values and achievements of past generations; and (3) a mediator between the culture and the individual. Isn't this being rather—what should I say—grandiose? Isn't it too much of a burden to lay on a little textbook?"

I've begun shaking my head even before she's finished speaking. "Not at all!" I protest. "A philosophy text for children should be representative of the thinking that has historically been the case in the discipline of philosophy. It really doesn't take much to trigger the reader's reconstruction of the traditional arguments: a snippet of Heraclitus here, or Duns Scotus Erigina there, or Jean-Paul Sartre somewhere else. Pretty soon you have a patchwork quilt—or if you like, a mosaic—which children delight in opening up for discussion the way puppies delight in having a tug-of-war over an old shoe."

"But shouldn't the teacher be the primary mediator between the ethical and social values of the culture and those of the child?"

I stare at the sentence in the outline. "I guess you've got a good point," I acknowledge. "Maybe this item belongs better in part III, because what I think I'm really trying to say here is that the entire community of inquiry in the classroom—inclusive of the teacher—should provide a buffer between the culture and the child and not just the teacher alone. Of course, the community need not serve just as a

buffer; it can also fill the more traditional role of serving as an accultu-
rating agency."

"A little while ago, we were comparing the intrinsic interest of an
object that didn't contain reflection within itself with that of an object
containing such reflection. Could you tell me a bit about how you see the
differences between a text qua novel and an ordinary expository text?"

"There are many differences," I say, "but I'll just mention one or
two. I think the primary aim of the ordinary text is coverage. It takes a
particular subject-area, breaks it up into parts, and then deals succes-
sively with those parts."

"The survey approach."

"Right," I agree, "the survey approach. For the student to absorb
all this information and hold it together requires an expenditure of
considerable intellectual energy. The text qua novel, on the other hand,
approaches the subject-area intensively and qualitatively rather than
extensively and quantitatively. Moreover, the novel, as one reads it,
develops a cumulative power, a momentum, of its own. Before long,
instead of draining energy out of the reader, it imparts energy back in.
The novel, as the cognitive psychologist Marilyn Adams has noted, can
be a powerful schema that interconnects and compounds meanings
cumulatively, whereas the expository text is condemned to chug along
always in its inert, linear fashion."

"Okay!" Natasha says, although it would have taken little encour-
agement from her to have me continue. "I'd like to go on now to part I,
item 6.b in your outline: the oral reproduction of the written text."

"What about it?" I ask. "The kids just read it aloud, paragraph by
paragraph."

"Yes, but what's the significance of their doing so?"

"Well," I say, "one bit of significance is to be found in the fact that
it forces them to alternate reading and listening. If they want others to
listen to them, they have to listen to others. This kind of reciprocity has
important ethical implications."

"Yes, so I see from part I, item 6.a," Natasha remarks, a bit tartly.
"But what else?"

"I see it as the beginnings of a shared experience, the beginnings of
a sharing of meanings. The text is presented to them without explanation. In fact, it is offered to them as a story, with no strings attached,
and this encourages them to invent stories of their own and offer them
in return."

"By taking turns reading the story, you think that they appropriate it?"

"Stories, to children, are precious commodities — spiritual goods," I insist. "They are the kinds of goods we deprive no one of when we make them our own. Children love the fictional characters in the stories they read: They appropriate them as friends — as half-imaginary companions. By giving children stories to appropriate and meanings to share, we provide children with other worlds to live in — other realms in which to dwell."

Natasha sniffs. "Surely you don't mean that your fictional texts are escape literature?"

"To some extent they may well be," I respond. "But I see them more as empowering the child in this world, rather than just offering a way of fleeing to the next. It's all very well to encourage children to fantasize about magical universes that don't exist, but I'd like to help them use reason to discover how extraordinary and uncanny the world is that they do inhabit. And funny."

"And funny?"

"Yes, it's so full of anomalies and discrepancies and contradictions because it's pushed together in the strangest ways. Like the other day, I read about this little girl who asked her mother, 'If I'm in love, do I have to stay home from school?' 'Why, no,' her mother replied, 'why do you say that?' 'Because my teacher told us today that love is contagious.' The child isn't aware of the ambiguity, of course, but neither are we in the case of most jokes, which are built on the same principle. We get suckered into one line of reasoning and then are surprised and amused to learn that another, equally good line of reasoning is the one that's applicable."

"So should humor be an essential element in the curriculum?"

"Absolutely!" I say emphatically. "A school without humor is like a diet without seasonings. No wonder children find schooling obnoxious, unless they can figure out how to make it play and fun."

"Is philosophy play and fun?" Her voice is low but gritty.

"It's cognitive play and cognitive fun. Good thinking may not always be hilarious, but it moves close enough to the edge of absurdity to make it exciting and amusing."

Natasha gazes out the window at the pattern of light and shadow on the lawn. "I'm thinking of that little girl. In the early part of the story we're puzzled by her inference that someone in love would have to stay home from school. Then, everything becomes clear: It's a perfectly reasonable inference if one first assumes that 'contagious' is to be understood literally."

"Yes, first we wonder and then we're surprised by understanding."

"And yet," Natasha muses, "it sometimes works the other way, doesn't it? I mean, sometimes we think we understand and then suddenly we're shocked and surprised, so that we're left in a state of wonder. That's why the parable is just the reverse of the joke."

"In the joke, we begin by being perplexed, then suddenly everything becomes intelligible, while with the parable it's vice versa?"

"Yes, I'm thinking of Tolstoy's parable of the three dimwitted hermits. You know, the bishop spends the whole day with them teaching them the Lord's Prayer. It is evening before he can return to his ship. Then he sees lights coming across the water. It's the three hermits, running on the surface of the ocean. 'Bishop, bishop!' they cry out, 'we've forgotten the prayer!'"

"Reversals are important in logic because they're important in how we think and in how we act," I acknowledge. "That's why Aristotle made them essential to tragedy, which, for him, rests on an unexpected reversal of the hero's fortunes."

Our conversation dissolves into silence.

At length I remark, "You know, I'd just like to come back to Vygotsky for a minute. He's got such a restless mind — you can tell it as you read him: He's always thinking!"

Natasha responds, with a touch of irony, "Also, his thoughts are consecutive. He doesn't jump around like a grasshopper."

I stare stonily at the green plant hanging from the ceiling. "Any reference to present company, living or dead, is purely coincidental, no doubt!"

Natasha shrugs. "I didn't intend it as a judgment of better or worse. I was simply commenting on contrasting styles of thinking. It can be understood as an order ranging from smoothly continuous to abruptly discontinuous."

"Oh, right!" I agree. "Vygotsky discusses the smoothness of mental functioning as an area in which he disagrees with Piaget . . . "

She interrupts, " . . . who based his position on the experimental work of Claparède . . . "

" . . . whose conclusions, in turn, were similar to those of Nietzsche, for whom negation preceded affirmation. Claparède claimed that awareness of difference precedes awareness of similarity. Piaget uses this notion to argue that children are compelled to devise logic — such as the making of logical distinctions — in order to enable them to cope with the frustration they experience when they fail to function adequately in the world of adults."

"This interests you?"

"Well, yes. I mean, what interests me is not so much how these awarenesses originate as the significance their emergence holds for the construction of logic."

"But isn't that what Piaget and Vygotsky are trying to explain?"

"Perhaps, but not exactly in the way I mean." I open Vygotsky's *Thought and Language* to page 88, glance at it for a moment, and then continue. "If we agree with Vygotsky and Davydov that the psychological history of the individual is in some ways 'commensurate' with the social history of the species, then it could be that these early efforts by the child to organize the awareness of similarity and difference into a general framework of logical understanding are commensurate with the efforts by philosophers to organize the earliest systems of logic."

Natasha regards me soberly. "But how could you show that?"

"By reference to the very first few pages of Aristotle's *Prior Analytics*, in which he discusses both the principle of conversion and the nature of propositions."

"You mentioned conversion earlier, when talking about the importance, in human experience, of reversals, turnabouts, total contrasts . . . "

"Yes," I interrupt, "the sort of fundamental changes that the yin–yang symbol expresses. Anyhow, there is a sense in which the awarenesses of similarity and difference are basic in human experience, and there is a sense in which the four propositional forms cited by Aristotle are basic in classical logic."

"Your point, I take it, is that there is a correspondence between these awarenesses and these propositions?"

"Correct," I reply. "Two of the propositional forms are canonical examples of distinction-making: *No X are Y* and *Some X are not Y*. The other two propositional forms are canonical instances of connection-making: *All X are Y* and *Some X are Y*."

"But surely this is nothing new!" Natasha exclaims. "Don't most approaches to the teaching of cognitive skills begin with the making of comparisons, and isn't it comparison that we are talking about when we speak of awareness of similarity and difference?"

I nod agreement. "That is certainly the case. But our earliest school curriculum, *Elfie*, actually begins by introducing the logical foundations and the psychological foundations together."

"And does that strategy continue — that at every successive stage of development, there is a correspondence in your program between the logical and the psychological? I should have thought, if you were guiding yourself by Vygotsky, that the teaching would *precede* the development of the child!"

"That is certainly the case. We use narrative philosophy to model the cognitive development of the child, not simply to create a one-to-one correlation between the psychological stage and the logical. What is of even more importance is to present the logic in a way that unfolds rationally. We then encourage the child's development to mirror that rationality."

Natasha stands and begins to put on her coat. "This," she says, "is something I'm going to have to think about on the bus."

FOURTH VISIT

My wife, Teri, hands me the phone when it rings, saying merely, "It's for you."

It's Natasha. Already, only a day after her last visit?

"Sorry to bother you," she says rather brusquely, "but we're not moving fast enough. I've taken on another project, to start next month, in Argentina, so I've got to finish this one up."

"As you like," I tell her. "Would you like to come on Monday?"

"I'll be there Monday," she says and hangs up.

Teri and I exchange raised-eyebrow glances.

*   *   *   *

Despite the steadily falling snow, which had started at midnight, she arrives Monday, just a few minutes late.

"I could have driven down to the bus stop and picked you up," I say apologetically.

"It's no trouble," she responds. "I love walking in the snow."

It is something for me to keep in mind: Natasha seldom wastes words.

She chases the cat off the chair she generally sits in and settles down with her notebook.

"Moving right along," I murmur.

Her eyes narrow suspiciously for a moment, as if it has crossed her mind that I may be making fun of her somewhat peremptory mannerisms. I now regret my blithe comment, but there is no way of taking it back.

"I've been thinking about what you said at the end of our last meeting," she begins, "and I've been wondering what you meant when you said that logic must be presented in a way that unfolds rationally, so as to encourage the child to emulate that rationality." She has said all this in a very composed and businesslike way, and now she suddenly laughs, her eyes merry, and she adds, "What does this mean?"

I take a moment to cross my legs and another moment to clasp my hands over my knee. Still another moment goes by as I bite my upper

40

lip. All of this acting out goes on while I struggle to decide how to begin. She continues to observe me steadily, and her pencil continues taking down notes. I feel like I'm on a slide under a microscope.

At length I say, "As I've already told you, when I wrote *Harry* I took it for granted that Piaget was right about 11 to 12 years of age being the beginnings of the so-called formal stage and, therefore, the appropriate period in which to begin helping children to find out about formal logic."

"Do you now think he was mistaken?"

"I understand there's now a great deal of skepticism about whether most people ever reach the formal stage. At the same time, there are some for whom logic in the form of the syllogism can be introduced much earlier — say, around age 8. And informal logic can be introduced when children are just beginning to talk."

Natasha grins. "Like helping the toddler with her notion that the children may have to stay home from school because love is contagious."

"Anyhow," I continue, "about 12 years after I'd written *Harry*, it occurred to me that I ought to be preparing the curriculum for the early elementary years leading up to *Harry*. I decided to work backwards, starting with 9- and 10-year-olds and descending toward kindergarten."

"*Must* the curriculum be written backward?"

"No, not at all," I reply quickly. "Our secondary school curriculum ascended step by step from the *Harry* stage on. But with *Harry* already in place, a step-by-step descent seemed very appropriate. See, there are things in *Harry* that the characters discover and discuss — like the rules of reasoning. But what a *rule* is, they take for granted. They talk about individual things being members of classes, but they take for granted what a *class* is. It is these things, which function in *Harry* as primitive or undefined terms, that I decided needed to be examined in the book just prior to *Harry* — the one that turned out to be *Pixie*."

"And *Pixie* opens up rules and classes and relationships and analogies, but takes for granted — what?"

"Well, statements and similarities and differences. Basic units of experience and basic units of meaning."

She mulls over what I have been saying, her pencil clamped sideways in her mouth like a horse's bit. Finally, she remarks, "And so the end result — the sequence of curriculum units from kindergarten to grade 6 — forms a logical sequence?"

"Yes, logical in the sense that an inverted pyramid is coherent and logical. Like the strong man in a circus who holds two men on his shoulders and these two hold three more on their shoulders."

Her brow furrows. "I don't understand."

"What I mean is, Elfie discovers that things have relationships. Pixie discovers that relationships have relationships and form analogies. Harry discovers there is a transitive structure to reasoning, enabling him to construct valid arguments. And all the while these logical discoveries they are making are being put to work in practical, everyday applications. So the pyramidal structure is both logically organized and rationally applied."

"This is what makes you think that you are strengthening the judgment of the children who take philosophy?"

"It's one of the reasons. There are others equally good or better."

For the briefest of moments, I discern a flicker of the Mona Lisa smile. Then the business-as-usual mask returns.

It is at this moment that the phone rings — for her, not for me. Her conversation consists almost completely of anxious, inquisitive monosyllables: When? How? Why not? and the like. The interchange ends almost as soon as it had begun. She puts down the phone and hurries to the closet to get her long winter coat and her enormously long scarf. "I must catch the bus back to New York immediately," she says to me.

"Get in my car," I tell her. "That's the only way you'll make it."

She doesn't protest and instead offers an explanation. "My son is ill. I left him with my father."

The bus pulls into the bus stop with us right behind it. In an instant, she has boarded it and is gone.

*   *   *   *

Several times over the next few days, I think of calling to find out how her son is, but each time I put it off. I can't say exactly what my reason is for not doing so, but I guess one factor is that we had tacitly agreed to establish a line between us that made our relationship professional rather than personal. She had been forced to cross that line. It would not do now for me to use that fact as an excuse to violate the agreement deliberately.

And then, as coincidence would have it, I receive a phone call from Boris. Now, I've known Boris for a great many years. He's what used to be called a "teacher trainer," although that phrase now sounds pejorative, so such people are more often called "teacher educators." The moment he tells me he has read the news release about my visit to Moscow, I have a suspicion about why he is calling. Boris, I have been told by a mutual acquaintance, had recently been to Georgia to attend

a conference conducted by Amonashvili on "humanistic education." I
have read Amonashvili's *Hello, Children* and it sounds ever so much like
the affective education that ruled the roost in the United States of the
1960s.

Boris and I had never talked much about his version of humanistic
education, although I can remember ending one conversation with the
remark that if it was the truth, it was still a long way from being the
whole truth. As for his view of me, it was that the only thing I was
concerned with in education was the furtherance of critical thinking.

So he has called now, in order to regale me with an account of his
exploits in Georgia, but we successfully stay away from topics that
might prove arguable or abrasive. Then I mention to him that I am
working on a research project with a freelance writer from the Soviet
Union.

"Oh?" he says, more out of politeness than curiosity, "what's his
name?"

When I tell him, there is a silence at the other end of the line. He
then asks me where she is now. I explain about her son's illness.

"Matthew!" Boris thunders at me. "Her name's not Natasha, she's
not a freelance writer, she has no children, and her father was killed at
Smolensk!" With that he mutters an apology and hangs up. When I try
calling him back, I get no answer.

*   *   *   *

Waiting for Natasha — if that was indeed her name — to appear for our
regular Thursday morning meeting, I resolve not to bring up Boris's
allegations. It is not inconceivable that Boris is mistaken — or possibly
he is lying, for what reason I have no idea. As for Natasha, I have to
admit that the details she has provided me with are fuzzy, but I have a
clear sense of her integrity. Still and all, I reason, that "clear sense"
could itself be wrong.

There is no way I can think of in which I can verify or falsify Boris's
claims. One thing that troubles me — or rather, encourages me to think
he might be wrong — is his statement that her father had been killed at
Smolensk. Now, Smolensk is a big city and no doubt lots of people get
killed there every year. But if he meant that Natasha's father had been
killed in the battle of Smolensk in World War II, that would make her
about 46 or 47 years old and that was obviously wrong.

There is no time, however, for further such reflections. Natasha
appears and is ready to resume our conversation as if nothing had
happened.

"Before we go back to Davydov," she begins, "I want to ask you something else about the need for what you call a 'rational curriculum.' Why do you think this is something needed in education? Is it because the different subject-areas taught during the school day appear to students to be disconnected and fragmentary . . . "

" . . . with the result that they are meaningless? Absolutely. But more than that," I go on, warming to a topic I had talked about many times before, "each particular subject-area should be more than just a heap of information, to be doled out scoop by scoop, day after day. Each subject should unfold, build on itself, question itself, illuminate itself from within, and build bridges with its fellow disciplines. And the only way this can happen is to use the narrative rather than the expository method. After all, what is most important is not that the teacher achieves coverage, but that the students acquire the meanings that are available in the subject-matter."

She raises her hand. "Enough! I get the point." She crosses out something she had written and hastily scribbles in something else.

"Back now to VVD?" I inquire.

"Back to VVD," she agrees, sighting along her pencil at me. Then she adds, "From what you've read of Davydov, what would you say is his central theme — the one he always comes back to?"

I mull her question over for a few moments, then reply, "Well, they're all interconnected you know. It's hard to talk about development without talking about teaching or consciousness or activity or the role of theory and abstraction, as he construes these topics."

"Are you saying, then, that it doesn't matter where we begin?"

"No, it does matter. Some ways into a situation are better access routes than others."

"Do you think the study of Davydov will enable us to rectify some of the misconceptions people have had about Vygotsky and Piaget?"

"I hadn't thought of it that way. Why, is that how you see the purpose of our inquiry?"

Natasha's smile is fleeting and enigmatic. "Doesn't someone in *1984* say that whoever controls the past controls the future, and whoever controls the present controls the past?"

"As an example of transitive reasoning, it's an innocuous remark; as an example of political reasoning, it's monstrous."

The wintry smile reappears. "But perhaps a grain of truth? Perhaps a half-truth?"

I feel that I'm being taunted and am reluctant to rise to the bait. "Let's get back to your question about a main idea in Davydov. I suggested that there was a conceptual network involved, rather than a single main idea."

"Would you say the same thing about Vygotsky?" she inquires.

I riffle through some notes I have made on Vygotsky and, at the same time, turn the question around and around in my mind. "Maybe not," I say at last. "Vygotsky's greatest idea was the ZPD—the zone of proximal development. All his discussions of inner speech and outer speech, concreteness and abstraction, consciousness and self-conscious-ness, monologue and dialogue—they all lead to this epoch-making un-derstanding of how the quality of education is to be improved through a recognition that children are at their best when engaged in cogni-tive cooperation with their peers and mentors, while they are at their least effective when isolated from any form of cognitive commu-nity."

"Have Western psychologists been receptive to the concept of the ZPD?"

"I think so—more than any other idea of Vygotsky's. Not only because it lends itself to experimentation, but because it helps resolve some nagging theoretical issues as well."

"Such as . . . ?" she asks.

"Well, take the distinction between competence and proficiency—a pretty canonical distinction among our psychologists. Competence represents universal aspects of development—like beginning to crawl and beginning to walk. Proficiency represents more individualized as-pects of development; supposedly competence is a precondition for proficiency. Nevertheless, psychologists have been troubled by a slew of cases in which people have apparently developed specialized profi-ciencies without having reached the requisite level of competence. The theory of proximal development makes such cases much more readily understandable."

Natasha nibbles on her pencil. "There are also," she says, "the polar bear and the skunk. Like Isaiah Berlin's hedgehog and fox."

"The polar bear and the skunk . . . ?"

"The polar bear has many big ideas. The skunk has only one idea and that is very, very small." Her eyes are hooded and round as mar-bles.

"So how would you categorize your Soviet psychologists?"

"Vygotsky is a polar bear; Davydov seems to be a fox," she says with a chuckle.

It is my turn to ruminate. Finally, I say, "I'll suspend judgment on them. But I see Mead as definitely a hedgehog and Dewey and Peirce as definitely polar bears." Natasha surveys me with a sly grin, as if I have allowed a pro-American bias to assert itself. But she does not translate the meaning of the grin into words. "In any event," I add, "I've made up my mind: The conceptual area most frequently dealt with by Davydov is that of the role of abstraction and theory. If we assume that frequency of reference is a criterion of importance—of the way he ranks in importance the topics he deals with—then that's where we should turn next."

"I have no preference," she says with a nod. Her face, likewise, reveals neither approval nor disapproval. Half under her breath she says, "You're beginning to sound like a book again."

"What kind of book?"

"A textbook."

"Maybe," I respond, "I sound like one because I am one. But you'll not escape reciprocity. You sound like a book too—like a novel."

She reddens. "Thank you. That's the nicest thing anyone has said to me all week. And perhaps, too, I sound like one because I am one."

You are a textbook, you are a novel: How quickly dialogue moves to metaphor and how swiftly metaphor moves to metaphysics! Is metaphor what Nelson Goodman says it is, a statement that is literally false but figuratively true? Or is it, more plausibly, what Donald Davidson and other have claimed—an ambiguous expression that is true in a narrow but profound sense and equally true in other senses that are less narrow but less profound?

I try to concentrate on assembling in my mind the cluster of concepts that Davydov employs to deal with the notion of abstraction, but my mind is clouded by recollection of Boris's accusations. After a struggle, I say, "As I understand him, Davydov is trying to get us to see that it is pedagogically wrong to emphasize, as Piaget does, the concrete character of the experience of the child entering school. Such children must, as Davydov puts it, 'begin to perform learning activities in order to master knowledge and skills that are in some way linked with the theoretical thought of their times.'"

"Skatkin used to say," Natasha muses, "that 'the very object of cognition is mediated by knowledge' (in Davydov, 1988c, p. 20). So, presumably, Davydov is convinced that if you feed the child only empirical knowledge, the child can perform only empirical actions. Deprived of theoretical concepts, the child cannot perform the actions that correspond to such concepts" (ibid.).

"So the two generations of children who have been brought up according to Piagetian principles have been conceptually undernourished and abstraction-starved and this, in turn, helps account for their lack of success in their later education. Yet we continue to blame the teachers for the miseducation our children receive!"

"You're indignant."

"Of course I'm indignant!" I growl. "Aren't you?"

"Whatever happens, happens as it must and could happen in no other way. If things are historically determined to happen as they do, there's no point in getting emotionally worked up about them."

"These are empty pronouncements because there's no way of falsifying them," I snap. "You can't prove to me that things could not have happened otherwise."

"Nor can you prove to me that they could have."

I feel tricked and trapped. I feel Natasha has led me into one of those dilemmas that the followers of Kohlberg use. A predicament is cited in which only two alternatives are possible, and these cancel each other out. Reason is thus made helpless and the psychologist is free to observe how the individual would react purely on the basis of his or her nonrational impulses (as though this reaction would somehow represent the true nature of that individual).

"I am determined," I begin, with heavy deliberation, "I am determined to return to Davydov. He is saying that children exposed only to specific materials can learn only specific modes of dealing with such materials. If we want to encourage them to grasp general modes of action, we have to introduce them to abstract materials" (1988d).

"This is the famous 'ascent from the abstract to the concrete.'"

"It's a misleading formulation," I suggest. "What Davydov is really arguing is that if we encourage the child's immediate, concrete experience to be mediated by abstractions, then the child will eventually achieve that desirable union of 'knowledge about' and 'acquaintance with' that James and Russell talk about."

"Is there, like, a ladder or something that enables us to move from the conflict between thesis and antithesis on up to the synthesis?"

"Pardon me?"

"I mean," she says, "you begin with a thesis of knowledge without experience and a counterthesis of experience without knowledge. You want to transcend this opposition, I take it, and move to a synthesis of experience that is simultaneously concrete and understood."

"So you're asking is there a ladder by means of which the ascent is to be made, and if so, what are the rungs?"

Natasha nods, her pencil poised.

I frown as ferociously as I can. "Davydov has a list, but I'm not sure it's a list of rungs. It's more like a list of what used to be called, in the educational jargon of the 1970s, 'behavioral objectives.' They go something like this:

1. *Precedence of the general over the particular.* Abstract knowledge precedes acquaintance with particular concrete items of knowledge. Pupils share the general knowledge but deduce the particular. Thus we all know, abstractly and in general, that stealing is wrong. But if you attempt to take my coat, I call it stealing, and by inference I conclude that it is wrong.

2. *Epistemology of the disciplines.* Pupils analyze the conditions under which the knowledge in a particular school discipline originated and came to be essential. Thus, to understand Darwin's theory, one would have to understand the circumstances that led to the theory's formulation.

3. *The essential definition of the object of knowledge.* Pupils must learn how to identify or discern the essential relationship that defines the content and structure of the object of knowledge. For example, if the object of knowledge is a glove, it is not enough to define it in terms of what all gloves — and only gloves — have in common; one must also explain how gloves are made. If the object of knowledge is a tooth, the formal definition is insufficient: One must also state how teeth come into being.

4. *Translation of defining relationships into various modes of expression.* Pupils should be able to reproduce the defining relationships of the objects they study in the form of graphic models, literal models, and so on. One can construct a graph depicting changes in the rate of glove production; one can write an essay about modes of glove-making; one can paint a picture of glove-makers at work; one can even make a pair of gloves oneself.

5. *Translation from universal to particular and from particular to universal.* Students should be fluent in making these transitions back and forth. Based on the observation of frequent uniformities, one can generalize responsibly. Likewise, based on inductively well-founded generalizations (universals), one can offer particular examples or illustrations.

6. *Translation from mental acts of overt acts and from overt acts to mental acts.* In effect, students should become adept at internalization *and* externalization. That is, they should be able to perform in thought what their peers are performing in dialogue and vice versa. (1988d)

Davydov goes so far as to claim that the mode of ascent from abstract to concrete is the essence of the dialectical-materialist world view. He sees it as being characteristic of all higher-order thinking, such as artistic, moral and legal thought. To teach children to move intellectually in this fashion is simply to have them learn the way scientists learn, using abstractions, generalizations and theoretical concepts."

Throughout this long disquisition, Natasha has been quietly taking notes and not even lifting her head to give me one of her chilling, challenging stares. Now she slaps her notebook shut, pouts, and looks at me over the tops of her reading glasses. "What do you think of items 2 and 3?" she asks.

"They're okay. When I was a student, Ernest Nagel used to make scathing attacks on genetic accounts of knowledge, in favor of what he called a functional account. And he was very persuasive. Nevertheless, Dewey continued to advocate a 'genetic-functional' approach and Buchler seemed to be arguing for an approach that would be not merely logical *and* historical, but *cumulative* as well."

Natasha tosses her head restlessly. "But are any of these, including Davydov, arguing that to understand a thing one has to *reenact* the way it came into being?"

"That's the position associated with Vico, and maybe there's something of the same kind in Hegel as well. Wasn't that the source of the *Verstehen* movement? Charles Taylor traces it back to Herder and Humboldt."

"I don't know," she says flatly. "I guess what I'm trying to find out—and I'm not being very successful—is whether you believe there are many ways of knowing or just one *right* way of knowing."

"Couldn't there be both? Couldn't there be many ways and the right way is the way that combines and coordinates all of them?"

She sighs. "All right, but could you give me an example?"

"If you'll accept another one from the children's curriculum."

"It's philosophy, isn't it? Vygotsky and Davydov—and Marx—were all trained as philosophers. So why shouldn't it be okay?"

"Very well, then," I say. "Here's what I would offer as an illustration—a passage for children aged 9 or 10, from *Kio and Gus*—and keep in mind that Gus is blind."

"Kio," I say, "my father and mother got me some real clay. I've already made a cat, like Roger. Do you want to try it out?"

"Sure," Kio says. I take him to my room and give him my clay cat.

"You make something!" I say to him.

"What should I make?" he says. "I know! I'll make a peach!" He rolls some clay in his hands until he has a round ball, then he gives it to me. "There!" he says. "A peach."

"That's silly," I answer. "Look, let me show you." I take a bit of clay and roll it into a little ball. "That's the pit," I say. Then I add some more clay around it.

"That's the part you eat," I say. And then I wrap another layer of clay around the whole thing. "That's the skin."

Kio says, "All I see is the skin."

"Sure, maybe that's all you *see*," I say, "but you *know* that what I made is really like a peach and *yours* isn't. Mine's a peach all the way through!"

Kio doesn't answer for a moment. Then he hands me some clay and says, "Make a head."

So I do, and I explain it to him while I work. "See, first I make the inside of the throat and the mouth. Then I put the tongue in. Then I add the teeth all around the gums. Then I put the lips over the teeth. Then I put the top on the head, push the nose out from the inside, and make the eyes with my fingernails. Then I add the hair and there it is."

"I start from the outside and you start from the inside," he says. I answer, "But you never *get* inside! You just *stay* on the outside! *That's* not the way to make a head!"

"It's the only way I know," Kio says.

"It *was* the only way you know," I answer. "Now you know *two* ways."

After reading the passage twice, Natasha stares meditatively at the cat sleeping in the other chair and remarks, "In Skatkin's book, *The Improvement of the Teaching Process*, pp. 37–38, he is critical of the standard approach to concept-formation. Take the concept of fruit, he says. It's not just a matter of abstracting and enumerating the external properties that are common to all fruits. Instead, one must examine the fruit in its interconnection with the whole plant, as an organic part of it. One must not just conceive of it statically, as logicians do, but in development, movement, and change."

"So for you, there is no human nature, only a history, which is the way Ortega put it."

She nods her agreement.

"And men, women, and children do not have their own specific natures, because they are all social inventions."

Again, she nods agreement. I wait, but she has no further comment on this point and I do not care to pursue it. At length, she says, "So there is Kio's way of knowing and there is Gus's . . . "

" . . . or, if you don't want to call them ways of knowing, call them styles of experience."

"They fall into oppositions that have to be transcended: the optic versus the haptic; men's versus women's; the logical versus the developmental; the experimental versus the intuitive; the analytical versus the empirical, and so on and so on."

"An assemblage of dialectical dichotomies," I comment, and then add, "I'm tired. Let's take a walk around campus — what do you say?"

The early morning sleet storm has encased the trees in crystal jackets and has covered the campus with a friable icing that crunches and crackles as we trudge over lawns and skitter perilously down paths. A bright winter sun has appeared and the lacy branches of the trees along the walks dazzle us with their glitter.

For all that, my mind is not on the resplendent scenery but on the unpleasant implications of Boris's phone call. Yet I refuse to consider the possibility that if Boris's allegations are correct, there might be something ominous in the wind. I prefer to think that it is somehow a case of mistaken identity.

The only point about which I do feel somewhat aggrieved is an aesthetic one: The whole thing sounds like it has been taken from a fourth-rate Russian novel. Even the names — Boris and Natasha, no less — are stagy and stereotypical!

Nevertheless, I can detect in myself a tiny, gnawing, nagging corner of concern. If Natasha isn't who she says she is, then who is she and why is she here? I recall that she offered few credentials when she first contacted me, but then reporters seldom do. If her identity and mission are not what they purport to be, what are they really? And how can that reality justify such an elaborate concealment?

Fully determined not to pry, I ask her — out of the blue, as it were — if she has ever worked as a reporter on any of the Moscow newspapers. (So much for good intentions!)

"Yes," she says, "I was with *Izvestia* for several years."

"*The News*, right?"

"Right," she says with a smile and proceeds to collect some icicles from a shrub. "The Russian word for 'news' is *izvestia* and their word for 'truth' is *pravda*. One of our standard jokes in Moscow was that 'there is no truth in *The Truth* and there is no news in *The News*.'"

We walk on in silence, stopping only to allow her to pick up a small branch, the size of a walking stick, and begin whacking away at the icicles that are beginning to form, like so many tiny stalactites, from the branches of the trees on our route.

Once again I resolve to avoid overstepping the line between the professional and the personal and then, no sooner than I have done so, I find myself asking her, "How's your son?"

She laughs. "Much better, thanks." No further elaboration.

I ask myself how he could be better if he doesn't exist. Or, to put it another way, if she had a son, would he be better? I decide to share the philosophical playfulness. "I know a joke," I announce.

"You can tell it," she says.

"A boy invites a girl on a date — his first date, by the way — and she, in turn, invites him to have dinner first with her family. He decides to discuss the matter with his father. His father says, 'After dinner, the family will leave the two of you alone. You will engage in conversation. There are three possible topics: food, family, and philosophy.' Everything happens as the father foresaw. Sitting with the girl, the boy racks his brain for something to say about food. Finally, he asks, 'Do you like pizza?' The answer he gets is 'No!' What to say about family? He asks, 'Do you have a brother?' Same answer. He's now down to his last topic — philosophy. In desperation he asks her, 'If you *had* a brother, would *he* like pizza!'"

A wan smile flits across her face. It disappears as she breaks her stick against the trunk of a tree, then reappears. "That reminds me of something my father used to tell me. He said that during the war, at Smolensk, he and some other soldiers were in the trenches together during a heavy bombardment. The first soldier asks, 'Of all the places on the Eastern front, why did I have to be here at Smolensk?' The second asks, 'Of all the centuries in which to be born, why did I have to be born in the twentieth century?' The third asks, 'Why did I have to be born at all?' There is a moment, as the others take this question in. Then the first soldier says wonderingly, 'Not to be born at all — to how many people can that happen? I would say to no more than three or four in a thousand!'"

I return her wan smile and ask, "Your father was at Smolensk?"

"Yes."

"And he's now in New York?"

An instant before her eyes had been merry and mischievous; now they are suddenly stony. She answers my question with a nod and turns back in the direction of the Institute. I ask her to come inside for another chat, but she shakes her head and proceeds silently in the direction of the bus stop.

FIFTH VISIT

Natasha's bus is scheduled to arrive at 8:55. It is now 7:55. I tell myself that if there is any hanky-panky going on such as Boris has alleged, I have a responsibility to determine what it is.

I peck out Boris's number on the phone. Surely he is awake by now. But no, it is like having awakened a hibernating bear. No matter how many times I tell him my name, he keeps shouting "Who? Who?" into the phone.

Now, evidently, his mind has cleared and he yells *"Matthew!"* at me with his more characteristic heartiness.

"Boris," I tell him, "you've got to give me more information. You can't just make accusations and hang up."

"You mean about that woman who calls herself Natasha."

"Natasha, yes."

"Her name is Svetlana. She was married to a psychologist. He was much older than she. He was political. He disappeared. She was also a psychologist. She worked as a therapist. Some of her clients were top people in the Party." Each of Boris's statements is a heavily accented growl.

"So?" I exclaim. "So what? There's nothing damaging about any of this that you've told me. Why are you so upset?"

"Because, professor, you're so innocent, that's why I'm upset! Because you don't know how the KGB works! Because right now there are a hundred Natashas and Svetlanas doing just what she's doing, in every major country, in every major profession! Matthew — how do they say, the young people? — *get real!*"

"Boris, you maniac," I tell him, "I ask you for evidence about Natasha and all you do is make accusations — without evidence — against a hundred other people! Please — until you have some facts to show me, don't bother me about this matter again."

"You called *me*, my friend," he says slowly and menacingly. His phone clicks dead.

*   *   *   *

Some people can't seem to put the cold war behind them, I tell myself, as I fidget at the typewriter, waiting for Natasha to show up.

53

Her scheduled time of arrival comes and goes. It must be that her bus is late, I reason. When she gets here, I think, no more of this Sherlock Holmes stuff. Back to the ascent from the abstract to the concrete.

She has hardly gotten her coat off when I ask her how long she's been doing freelance work.

If she is disturbed by my question, she doesn't show it. "Five years," she responds. Then she says, "Look, I've been meaning to tell you something about that. It's true I'm a freelance writer, but I'm also on contract from time to time, and that's what I'm on now."

"You mean you have a special assignment from some organization to come here and interview me?" I hold my breath.

"Yes." Extracting information from her can be like extracting teeth. To coin a phrase.

"May I ask who?"

"Of course! It's the *Guang Ming Daily* in Beijing. It's one of the larger papers in China."

I'm stunned. "Why would a Chinese newspaper send someone half-way around the world to talk to me?"

"The Chinese have always been interested in the education of the young."

"I'm aware of that. Why else would they have brought Dewey to China to speak to them about education?"

A wintry smile. "They weren't really interested in taking Dewey's advice. They just wanted to understand his thinking."

"I thought his China lectures, which were reprinted not long ago, were quite good. Not vintage Dewey, perhaps, but brisk and to the point. One thing he said that particularly sticks in my mind—because I don't believe he said it anywhere else—was that Aristotle's invention of logic was the greatest individual intellectual achievement in human history." I conclude lamely, "A fact more relevant to other of my concerns than to this conversation." I struggle to get back on track. "Just why did they want to understand Dewey's thinking?"

"The impression they had formed of Dewey—an impression fostered by Hu-Shih and Lin Yu-Tang—was that he advocated the liberation of the young. Cognitive liberation: the right of all children to think for themselves. The Chinese leaders pretended to by sympathetic, but, in fact, they were appalled. Throughout the twentieth century, they have been fascinated by this danger."

"What danger?"

"The danger that masses of young people would assert their intellectual freedom, which would, in turn, ignite a new revolution."

"So the Red Guards were like a nightmare come true?"

"Yes, but the Red Guards weren't a symbol of cognitive liberation, even though they were young. The same could not be said about Tienamen Square."

"You mean the real purpose of having Dewey come to China was to find out how young people think?"

"It was to find out how young people could be *made* to think. They figured that if anyone could tell them *that*, it would be Dewey. They figured he would never suspect their motives."

"I remember Santayana writing somewhere, in his elegantly malicious way, 'Dewey is a *good* man!'" I add, "So their policy amounts to psychological warfare against the young!"

Natasha shrugs. "Why are you surprised? That policy is neither new nor particularly Chinese. It's global."

"But surely you don't support it?"

She remains silent.

"Is there some weird sort of reciprocity here—having Dewey to China to find out how *he* thinks and your coming here to find out how *I* think?"

She looks at me soberly. "I am not a spy. I do not work for the government. I am a newspaper correspondent. Why are you shocked by what I'm doing? It's being done everyday and it's celebrated. If you're a novelist well past your prime, interview the astronauts' wives, find out how they think, and write a book about it. Is there a celebrated case about cold-blooded killers of an innocent family or someone who has just slaughtered his wife and children, then denied it—well, get friendly with the perpetrators, get inside their heads, as it were, and then tell the world what you've found there. Is there a dispute in the stately precincts of the Freud archives? Interview the psychiatrists and psychoanalysts in depth and then sell the interview to a popular magazine. This is what they do, in their grand way, and they are successful at it! Why can't I do something like it, in my small way, and be successful at it?"

"And I in mine," I respond. My thoughts are in too much disarray to permit me to proceed. I simply cannot take in and sort out all that Natasha has told me. Still, her revelations neither refute Boris's allegations nor confirm them.

"Back to the ascent from the abstract to the concrete, please," she says.

"Have we ever left it?" I inquire.

"Does Davydov ever give a specific example of going from the abstract to the concrete?"

"Well," I say, "I think that, for him, *anytime* he gives an example, that's just what he's doing—concretizing (Davydov, 1988d). But you want a specific instance—let me think. Oh yes—the replacement of letter-symbols by concrete numerical symbols on the basis of identified regularities, something he also identifies with the movement from the general to the particular" (ibid.).

"So when we instantiate $a = b^2$ with $9 = 3^2$, we're moving from the abstract to the concrete?"

"Yes, according to Davydov," I respond.

"What about according to you?"

"I've no problem with categorizing such instantiation as a move from the general to the particular or from the abstract to the concrete, but I think it's something else again to set this up as some kind of overall educational formula. I suspect that the mind of the child and the mind of the adult resonate in the same ways in these cases. Both oscillate constantly between generalizing and particularizing or exemplifying. The architecture of thinking has generalizing and specifying as two of its major structural features, just as Gothic architecture ascends skyward over the opposition of the two halves of the broken arch, to cite a dialectical example."

"Can you give me an example of its being better to proceed from the concrete to the abstract?"

"In the teaching of logic, it seems to me better to proceed from informal logic—the logic of practical reasoning with natural language in situations of everyday life—to formal reasoning using symbols instead of words. It's not that you can't move in the other direction—you can, but it may be uphill rather than downhill."

"Why's that?" she persists in asking.

"Because words are meaning-bearers and letters are content-free. When we reason with words and the logic works, the result is very gratifying. But when, in order to reason, we have to translate from words to symbols and then from symbols back to words, the two translation leaps we perform are so perilous that we cannot help having doubts about the validity of the overall process." I lean back in my chair, as if to indicate we can go no further on this point.

"Do you assume that the terms 'abstract' and 'concrete' are antitheses of one another?"

"I guess they're opposites in many respects, but that opposition can also be problematic. I mean, when Goldstein and Gelb (Goldstein, 1964) were studying what they called 'abstract' and 'concrete' behavior on the part of patients with brain injuries or brain lesions, they seemed to assume that reference to a genus is 'abstract,' while reference to a species of that genus is 'concrete.' That's a risky assumption, because genus and species are relative terms, and a term can be subordinate in one context and superordinate in another. Furthermore, it is not obligatory to equate thinking in terms of abstractions with 'higher-order thinking' and thinking in terms of concrete particulars with 'lower-order thinking.' For example, the patients of Goldstein and Gelb couldn't verbalize the word 'red' as that which a number of color samples had in common, but they could identify them individually as 'vermilion,' 'carmine,' 'scarlet,' and so on. That seems to me qualitatively at least as good as calling them all 'red' but not knowing what they are in each particular case. By the way, you seem to be tolerating my lectures much better."

"I'm learning to endure them much better, thank you."

"They're an occupational hazard, I'm afraid."

Natasha turns to a new sheet on her notepad, sighs, and looks at me inquisitively. "What do you think of Davydov's treatment of the move from the general to the particular?"

Once again, I tilt my chair back. Eventually I say, "Well, I'm really not sure. He says that children transform their generalizations into concepts that correspond to the 'kernel of the academic subject.' This puzzles me. Wouldn't such a concept, even if it's an accurate definition or explanation, still be abstract?"

"You said earlier," she remarks, shuffling through her notes until she comes to a page she wants, "that the 'concrete' Davydov is talking about — the concrete that is the goal of the ascent — is actually a combination of knowledge about and acquaintance with, as well as of knowing that and knowing how. So who is inconsistent here, you or Davydov?"

I try to be conciliatory. "I thought my earlier interpretation was a charitable one, true to his intent if not to his words."

"Then why not extend him the same courtesy here?"

"Very well," I acquiesce, aware of Natasha's capacity for persistent pursuit. "Let me go back over his unpacking of the components of a learning task that the teacher presents to the children:

1. *Analysis*. The factual material is analyzed to discover in it some general relationship that has a rule-governed connection with the various manifestations of that material;

2. *Deduction*. Having abstracted and generalized, the children deduce the particular relationships in the given material and their unification in the construction of the kernel — that is, of the concrete mental object; and

3. *Mastery.* Through this process of analysis and synthesis, the students master the general mode whereby the object under study is constructed" (Davydov, 1988c).

Natasha tilts her head to one side. "Do you still find this objectionable?"

"I find the word 'deduce' is being used in a peculiar way, but perhaps that's just a translator's problem, so I won't go into it."

Natasha's eyelashes flutter innocently. "Anything else?"

"I must confess I'm struggling here. I know this business about the need to master the 'general mode whereby the object under study is constructed' is important to Davydov. I asked him about it in the first conversation I had with him in Moscow, and he reemphasized it."

"So what do you *think* it is?" she murmurs.

"My best guess is that we need to look more closely at Davydov's key terms:

1. *Relationships.* Davydov says that the children first discover general relationships in the subject-matter, and then later they deduce particular relationships that they unify in order to construct the kernel — the concrete mental object. What I would stress here is that the relationships — such as similarity, difference, and identity — are discovered, not invented. They are then analyzed, through inquiry or reflection. They are consequently organized into a conceptual core that captures and expresses the origin and development of the object in question.
2. *Rule-governed.* I might substitute here the term 'logical.' That is, Davydov is arguing that there is a logical and not merely a contingent relationship between the relationships discovered in the subject-matter and the relations that comprise the conceptual core. The translation from existential connections to conceptual connections is governed by logical rules.
3. *Construction.* This term is used twice, but not in the same way. The first time, it refers to the construction of the conceptual core or kernel. The second time, it refers to the construction — that is, the development — of the object under study."

"I don't know whether this helps any or not," I add. "But there is no question about Davydov's seriousness in espousing the genetic method. He quotes a number of other writers — Kapterev, Izvol'skii, Shimina, and the 20th-century Russian neuropsychologist P. Y. Gal'perin (Davydov, 1988c, 1988d) — to back him up on this point."

"Gal'perin? What does he quote from Gal'perin?" She stares at me intently.

I read it to her: "Only in genesis is the genuine structure of mental functions revealed: once they have definitely taken shape, their construction becomes impossible to discern — more than that, it 'sinks out of sight' and is covered over with a 'phenomenon' that has a completely different aspect, nature and structure" (in Davydov, 1988d, p. 53).

"But Gal'perin is speaking here only of the importance of the genetic method for the study of *mental* functions and Davydov is talking about its importance for the study of *any* functions, whether mental or physical or whatever." She leans forward, her eyes narrowed.

"You're right," I reply. "But are you suggesting that the genetic method might be appropriate for the study of mental functions, just as Gal'perin claims, but inadequate for the study of other things?"

Natasha shrugs but says nothing.

"Or does this bring us around back to Dewey and his advocacy of a 'genetic-functional' method, as opposed to Nagel's 'functionalism?' I think Dewey was alive to the possibility that genetically oriented, historical, narrative-structured inquiries can get at the subject-matter in ways that are not open to other approaches."

Natasha's forehead is furrowed now, but she still doesn't put her puzzlement into words. As for myself, I have temporarily lost interest in what I was talking about, as I begin to wonder about the mysterious dynamics of the interview process, the complicated moves and countermoves, the swift alternation of highs and lows of feeling, and the teetering precariousness of the whole process, which at every moment may just manage to persist, or may just as well go smash. Being interviewed is a waste of time, I tell myself — an absurdity that we put up with only because we're such narcissistic egomaniacs. We should either stay away from it — as one would stay away from alcohol — or we should try to cut our losses by controlling the interviewer. But how does one do that — control the interviewer? That would be possible only if the interviewer were one's own invention. But this would be even more of an absurdity than the traditional interview . . . It is a wild thought, one that might have been proposed by Jorge Luis Borges, the Argentinian author of bizarre stories.

Natasha seems to be rousing herself from meditations of her own. Finally, she remarks, "In your novels for children, you place a good deal of emphasis on mental acts, which I suppose are like the mental functions referred to by Gal'perin. I remember that *Pixie* ends with talk about *knowing* and *Kio and Gus* begins with that kind of talk. Also, in your manuals, you have a lot of exercises aimed at getting kids to sort out mental acts, like you'll ask them to tell the difference between knowing and believing. By the way, how *do* kids answer a question like that?"

"Oh, they'll kick it around for a while and then someone will say something like, 'Knowing is accepting something as true that *is* true, while believing is accepting something as true that may be true or false.' But what are you getting at?"

"What I'm getting at," she says, "is that such questions get kids to provide the criteria with which a logical definition can be constructed. But in your novels, you don't *define* such mental acts as knowing, wondering, or believing. What you do, instead, is *portray coming to know* and *coming to wonder*. You show how Harry comes to doubt and how Millie comes to make distinctions and how Suki tries to explain to herself what meaning is."

"So?"

"I'm just citing it as an example of how the narrative method complements the logical or critical approach —"

" — the analytical approach —"

"Yes, I suppose that's what it would be called in philosophy. The analytical approach." She pauses to search for something in her mind, then announces, "All right, I think I have a definitive example. In the last chapter of *Suki*, where the class is discussing the meaning of meaning, Harry attempts to devise a formal, definitional approach, while Suki tries to develop an approach that is much closer to imaginative invention. Nevertheless, they recognize that their separate lines of inquiry tend to converge . . . Oh, that's what we were saying earlier, isn't it?"

I nod. I am content to let her talk if that is what she is of a mind to do. She raises her hand impatiently: "Let me show you! Let me have a copy of *Suki*."

I have a copy within reach, and I hand it to her without further comment. In her richly accented voice, she reads Suki's poem, which Suki claims is an effort to tell what meaning is:

As letters —
until words —
tell us nothing,
so a poem
is not in its words
but in their network.

Words and things interbreed
with each other

and with ourselves.
Their ways are
countless as numbers
and more prolific.

Merely connect,
and a further surge of current
sizzles along the grid.
The filaments of the mind
begin to glow:
possibilities constellate.

Of course, no one can know
the whole of a poem
or even one part
perfectly.

Poems,
for all that, are
the sense they make.

"Don't you see how it moves," she proclaims. "From words to relationships and from relationships to possibilities."

"So I've noticed," I respond, and her face responds, in turn, with a
twinkle of amusement. Then I add, "But there's something else there
that takes us back to the Davydov thing, and that's that the poem itself
illustrates the ascent from the abstract to the concrete. Look how it
begins with mere letters, which form words—words which are the initial bearers of meaning—and these words form a network of relationships, and these actual relationships portend innumerable possible relationships. But the whole thing, this whole process of development
and accrual, eventuates in that unification of perception, feeling, and
thought that we call sense."

"You connect it with Davydov," she says, "but I connect it with
Vygotsky. I'm reminded how, in the last two chapters of *Thinking and
Speech*, or *Thought and Language*, or however you translate the title of that
book into English, Vygotsky warns us against being reductionistic and
mechanistic. In our analysis, we should not reduce our subject-matter
to its separate elements, but to its smallest representative sample, in the
sense that, when we are considering the properties of water, we are
thinking of the H_2O molecule and not the separate properties of hydrogen and oxygen. Thinking and discourse are like hydrogen and oxygen.
Together they form a unit which is irreducible. To Vygotsky, that unit
is a unit of *meaning* and he identifies it with the word."

"Some philosophers, like Wittgenstein and Frege, might identify it instead with the proposition or sentence."

"But we're not talking about them," she says, almost querulously, "we're talking about Vygotsky and how what the poem says in the beginning about words is similar to Vygotsky's remarks about units of meaning."

"We've run on so long we've almost missed taking a break. What would you like — a walk, a ride, or both?"

"Another time," she says. "I've got to — how do you say it? — I've got to split."

I can't help being amused at her efforts to mimic the vernacular of younger Americans. "There's a little lake not far from here," I tell her. "Next town over: Verona. There's a nice path around it, and it's not such bad weather, really. Would you like to continue the conversation there?"

To my surprise, she agrees, and before long we are making our peripatetic way around the lake in Verona Park.

We walk past the boat house, now closed for the winter, and past the elegant little bridge, newly reconstructed, that throws itself across a tiny strait with all the panache that it might have if it were throwing itself across the Seine.

The fires of suspicion are banked now, as they are generally banked when Natasha is present. It is only in her absence that they flare up dangerously. I must learn to be more consistent.

"Natasha!" I say abruptly, "I find it difficult to believe — no, let me start again — why would a newspaper on the other side of the world send a correspondent to engage me in a series of interviews? Why me?"

"Why not?"

"I'm a small fish — a minnow, in fact!"

"The BBC thought your work important enough to make a one-hour film about it."

"If you only knew how pathetically tiny our publishing operation is and how few books we sell every year compared to the standard textbook publishing houses!" To myself I wonder, "How did I get started on this line of reasoning?" But to Natasha, I add, "We're really minuscule — although I suppose that's the way minnows are supposed to be."

She gives me a serious — if sidelong — glance and retorts, "It's not a question of quantity! Davydov and Rubtsoff didn't make an agreement with you because of the size of your operation. They think you may have a piece of the puzzle that's been missing."

"A puzzle has been missing?" My attempt at humor is lame.

"No!" she says, with some exasperation, "a *piece* of the puzzle has been missing!"

"And what do you understand that missing piece to be?"

"*Abstract content.*"

"Ah," I say to myself, "this is a game at which two can play!" So I say to her, attempting to assist her efforts to deliver her idea, "But 'abstract content' is a contradiction in terms!"

"So is 'philosophy for children'!" she fires back, undaunted.

"All right, so tell me, what's so important about abstract content?"

"Well," she says, relaxing enough to allow the corners of her mouth to curl up a bit. "Suppose we were to begin — as we were saying a few minutes ago — by taking as axiomatic 'the ascent from the abstract to the concrete.'"

"That's easy enough — sort of like presupposing that if two lines are parallel, they can never meet."

"Fair enough. But we ordinarily associate 'abstractness' with 'absence of content,' isn't that so?"

"Oh, I think you're absolutely right," I say. "People ordinarily cannot think of these two things in any way except as mutually exclusive. Okay — but so what?"

"Well, before I get to that, let me introduce another presupposition that people ordinarily make. If the goal is 'the concrete,' then this is something they associate with 'content-specific' thinking. And if the goal is content-specific, then the starting point must be content-free!"

"These are the assumptions people make. Okay. But what inferences do they then draw?"

"The inference has to do with the instruments to be employed in the zone of proximal development. The aim is to lift children's thinking from mediocre thinking to higher-order thinking. Such instruments, it is inferred, must themselves be content-free because the content-free is the abstract and the abstract is where we begin." She looks at me triumphantly, then looks away.

"This is why, then, the Piagetians are so big on having kids look at pages of dots to discover patterns in them — because the dots are thoroughly abstract and, therefore, thoroughly meaningless?"

"Exactly. What is so spectacularly unique about philosophy is that it is a content — indeed, a discipline — and, at the same time, it is both abstract and meaningful. Philosophy is the essential molecule of early elementary education, and abstraction and meaning are its two essential properties."

"You figured this out — ?"

I've no time to complete my question. "Don't be condescending, please," she shoots back. "You wouldn't talk that way to a child."

"I was just trying to say that I admired the way you thought this through."

"Please don't pay me any compliments," she retorts, looking straight ahead. "At the same time, don't get carried away by what I've been saying about elementary school philosophy as abstract content. There are lots of other problems I have with it, and it can still turn out to be some kind of mirage or illusion."

The conversation gutters and we attend for a while the sudden wheeling in the sky of a cloud of birds and the staccato friskiness of the ubiquitous squirrels. A tree leans perilously far out over the surface of the lake and as we pass it, we marvel at its daring.

I conclude, once again, that Natasha is a difficult person. I then revise my conclusion: We are inclined to find each other difficult. To myself, I think: "This is what you get for trying to be helpful!" But to her I say, "A moment ago you were talking about the 'instruments' to be employed in the zone of proximal development to lift the level of children's thinking. What sorts of instruments did you have in mind?"

"Anything people use to mediate between themselves and the world. Physicians and physicists use instruments this way. Instruments are located outside the individual—"

"—like tools," I offer.

"Yes, like tools. Nevertheless, as Vygotsky says, they are 'instruments of linkage'" (in Davydov, 1988e, p. 44).

"Right. And linkages are connections or relationships."

"And if relationships are meanings, instruments are meaning-generators," she says. She kneels to pick up a stone, then throws it at the surface of the lake. It drops in with a gentle plink.

"So would you say that concepts and symbols are also instruments and also serve to mediate between the individual and the world?"

"Certainly," she replies. "It's like Davydov says: A person correlates the singular through a series of mental actions; as a result, its meaning is derived from the links between those actions" (1988e, p. 44).

"I'm sorry," I interject, "I'm not following."

"Well," she says patiently, "Davydov is merely following Vygotsky's lead. Vygotsky claims that to know the meaning of a symbol is to apprehend the singular as the universal."

"So to know the meaning of the word 'dog' involves being able to look at a particular living, breathing, flesh-and-blood Rover and understand him generically—completely grasping what it means to be a canine."

"That's it," she says.

"Hmmm," I respond, "but while that takes care of my understanding the word 'dog,' it says nothing of whether I understand Rover. Can I ever know the mind of a dog the way I know the mind of another person?"

"Can you know the mind of another person?"

"In a sense — by analogy. From the three terms I know I can extrapolate the fourth. I know what I think and what I say as well as the relationship that exists between them. And I know what you say. So I reason that your thinking is to your saying as my thinking is to my saying."

"But what grounds do you have for assuming that the relationship between my thought and my speech is anything like yours?" she asks, her face alight. "And if the two relationships are not similar, your whole analogy crumbles!"

"Do you mean I can know your thoughts no better than I can know the mind of a bat? You seem to have little confidence in interpersonal understanding."

Natasha shrugs. "That needn't be the case at all. I wasn't questioning the truth of your conclusion — only the analogical tool you claimed to be employing for arriving at it."

We have arrived at a small dam at the upper end of the lake where a trickle of water flows down the face of the rocks, puddles for a moment at the foot of the dam, then spreads out and passes under the bridge on which we are standing.

By now we're thoroughly chilled. We hasten to the car and I take Natasha to the bus.

*   *   *   *

After reviewing with Teri the conversation I have had today with Natasha, I ask, "Am I wrong, Ter? Am I being abnormally suspicious? Have I any grounds for thinking that maybe I'm being used for purposes I would normally disapprove of?"

Teri looks up from her desk but doesn't put down her book. "I don't recall your thinking you were being used by the BBC."

"I didn't think I was and I still don't think so."

Teri grins. "They were only giving you your due, is that it?" When I fail to answer her mischievous question, she continues, "Perhaps that's all Natasha's doing." She returns to her perusal of George Herbert.

I'm not prepared to let the matter drop so quickly. "Is that what, ultimately, we're all afraid of—getting our due? That it would be like getting our comeuppance?"

Teri ignores my speculation and returns to the original issue. "I'm not saying your suspicions of her are groundless, but so far they seem to be pretty flimsy." She pauses, then adds, "I can't see any harm in playing it out. Are you learning anything?"

"Yes."

"So . . . " This time George Herbert commands her attention in earnest.

SIXTH VISIT

An icy wind sweeps the campus and as I look through my office window I see the small figure of Natasha struggling up the hill, while she attempts to shield her face with her executive briefcase. When she arrives at the front steps of the Institute, I note the addition to her usual apparel of a large beret, which is perched bravely, if precariously, atop her head.

Her fingers are too cold for note-taking, and she warms them on her coffee mug. "Sergei was a little difficult this morning," she tells me.

"Sergei is — ?"

"He is my son. He didn't want to go to school."

"What else is new?" I ask.

Natasha sighs. "I'm afraid I don't do a very good job of reasoning with him. But my father and he get along so well. They talked it over, and Sergei finally took himself off."

"Your father was in the war?" I blurt out.

"My real father was in the war. He was injured at Smolensk. After he died, my mother remarried. I call Maxim my father, but he is really my stepfather."

"And is Sergei really your son?" I ask, even as I think to myself, "Your questioning her like this is shameless — utterly shameless!"

Natasha laughs — a merry, tinkly little laugh. "Of course! And I suppose you now want to know all about the rest of my personal life, such as the name and whereabouts of Sergei's father, right?"

"Only if you want to tell me."

"I don't ask you questions about *your* private life."

"True," I concede, quite remorsefully.

"Well," she continues, "I wouldn't mind telling you, but I can't because it involves other people. Let me just say there was this man — he was a wonderful man and I still love him. Anyhow, I got involved with him but he couldn't marry me. At the time, I was writing about Bakhtin and Julia Kristeva on texts and he was doing some research on Vygotsky. Everything we talked about together seemed to leap to life, to become incandescent, and we talked together endlessly."

"Did he write about Vygotsky? Was it published?"

"What he wrote was never published. I read it. I thought it was brilliant. But —" she throws up her hands in a gesture of futility, "it was never published and now no one can find it." She is silent and meditative for a moment, then she adds, "He came by his interest in Vygotsky honestly."

"Oh? In what way?"

"Well, you may remember that Vygotsky had a colleague named E. V. Il'enkov."

"Of course! Davydov refers to him quite often. He was, in fact, a philosopher and he was Davydov's mentor."

"Right. This man I've been talking about — I'll call him Mikhail — was related to Il'enkov, although not in his immediate family, and he respected Il'enkov immensely, almost as much as he respected Vygotsky."

A dozen questions swarm in my mind, but I am prevented from asking any of them by a loud knock at the front door. I hurry to see who it is and find Boris slapping his hands together and stamping his feet. "Matthew!" he booms, after giving me a hug and ignoring the finger I place across my lips. "I've found out who she is. She's a correspondent for a Chinese paper. I was confusing her with her mother. But this information raises even more questions than it resolves —"

I finally manage to shut him up, hang up his coat and fur hat, and come into my office. They introduce themselves to each other. I'm certain Natasha has overheard Boris, but she acts as though she has heard nothing.

As they talk, I have a chance to study Boris, who reminds me (with my incurably cinematic memory) of no one so much as of Peter Ustinov as the Soviet submarine commander in *The Russians are Coming! The Russians are Coming!*

I am brought back to the conversation by noting a gleam in Natasha's eye, and I must admit that this is no happy reunion of old friends, even though they seem to be talking quite amicably. Natasha is being very careful, but she is prepared to do battle if she has to. More than that: She is prepared, if necessary, to carry the battle to Boris.

"So!" she says, when the tempo of the exchange has eased for a moment, "what do you think of Professor Lipman's work?"

Boris seems to choke a bit on his toasted bagel. Finally, he is able to gasp, "Charming. Utterly charming. Unbelievable."

Natasha unsheathes her talons ever so slightly. "Why don't you like it?"

Boris begins by blustering, but when he sees it doesn't take him very far, he becomes more serious. "It's just the wrong approach, that's all," he concludes.

"And what's the right approach?" she inquires, not relaxing her pursuit one bit.

"Well, you already know what I think the right approach is. It's Amonashvili and humanistic education. Matthew here seems to think that what's wrong with our educational system is that it's not *cognitive* enough, so he proposes to stuff it full of philosophy, the way one stuffs a carp or a goose. But what Amonashvili is saying is that the problem has been an *ethical* one. We haven't treated the child with respect, or with cooperation, or with love. The reform of education must begin with the reform of our attitudes!"

Natasha asks, "Actually, how familiar are you with the Philosophy for Children curriculum?"

Boris reddens. "I've read the whole of *Harry Stottlemeier's Discovery*! All that Aristotelian logic — ugh! It's completely wrong to force that sort of stuff on a child!"

Natasha glances at me as if to invite me to refute him, so I say, "There are some seventy chapters in the complete set of children's novels and of those seventy, only about six have to do primarily with formal logic and of those six, only three or four have to do with Aristotelian logic." As I speak, I wonder about Natasha's strategy. Is it to distract Boris from his preoccupation with her by setting him on me? Or is this simply a move in some larger strategy of hers?

Natasha turns to Boris once again. "Are you trying to reformulate the problem of education as one in which the cognitive and the affective are pitted against each other and the affective must triumph?"

"Absolutely yes," he says, slapping his hand on his knee.

"The Woodstock generation comes to the Soviet Union," I groan. "Boris, if you've paid any attention at all to what I've written, you'd know that I despise the split between the cognitive and the affective just as I despise the split between meaning on the one hand and perception and action on the other. I detest these Cartesian dualisms, and when children flee school, it's a sign that they detest them too."

"My friend," he says, knitting his enormous eyebrows together, "I did not come here today to argue with you. I wasn't born yesterday. I know what is going on. For example, I saw all three installments of the BBC trilogy: the one on Vygotsky, the one on Feuerstein, and the one on you — *Socrates for Six-Year-Olds*. Ugh, what a title!"

"What do you object to in them?"

"What do I object to in them? I'll tell you what I object to in them!

They're trying to turn this man Vygotsky into a saint! And the fact is that he was just an amateur in education, in philosophy, and in psychology. Look, how could a person try to—how do you say it?—to *vault* right to the top of a discipline when he's never taken any formal instruction in that discipline? Vygotsky never really studied psychology! He was not an insider. He was an outsider! He was not immersed in the system: He tried to make an end run around it and now he's being hailed as some kind of savior. And all because of that one crazy book!"

"That's all Spinoza had, too," I murmur.

"Another outsider," Boris retorts gruffly.

Natasha's voice is so even that I can't tell whether she's being ironic or not: "Those who work within the system are limited by one another. Each is sequestered into a tiny pocket and can only work within that pocket. Even those who, today, claim to be Vygotskians, are reproducing the system in their own activities by limiting themselves to microscopic studies that they feel will all link up together some day and vindicate their hero. But he needs little vindication. Those who count themselves in his camp, even if they don't count themselves his followers, must be prepared to set themselves dialectically over against the system, as he did, if something transcendent is ever to emerge from that confrontation. But from working within the system, virtually nothing will ever emerge."

Boris reaches across the table and tries to take her hand, but she pulls away. "Exactly!" he beams. "Exactly! One must be either outside or inside, and Amonashvili and I are inside. If purification is to be done, it must be done from the inside by those who have served loyally and diligently within the system. Yes, my dear, you're right: Our system is bureaucratic and is based on a division of labor. And that is why we cannot accommodate Vygotsky's holism. Education *must* be constructed of fragments—do you understand? It can never be a seamless whole. Matthew and Natasha, I beg of you, take your philosophers and your ideologues and your Quixotes and be off. Do not try to disturb arrangements that are deeply founded and profoundly wise. Nothing is to be gained by trying to confront the system, and the result can only be terribly harmful to the child."

"Boris," I remark, "you would make an outstanding Grand Inquisitor."

"You make a joke," he replies, "but I am serious."

Before I can say that I'm serious, too, he's up, says his goodbyes and departs.

As I resume my seat I say, "I'm sorry for the interruption. I had no idea he was coming." I say nothing about the allegations he has made about Natasha.

She looks at me soberly. "He's right, though," she remarks meditatively. "The educational system itself has an immune system and to it you represent a foreign body seeking acceptance. You may be tolerated for a while, but sooner or later you'll be rejected. For the present, you and it are incompatible."

"I'm resigned to the present," I respond. "I'm prepared to wait. I know that fads come and go in education. One day it's all microteaching and new math; the next day they've disappeared between the cracks. But philosophy in the elementary school is not a fad. It will haunt the system and give it bad dreams. Some day, when people are more ready for it, it will be incorporated without being rejected and without being made a travesty. Meanwhile, I accept my nonacceptance."

"Mikhail used to tell me that, too. I mean, about philosophy some day returning to the elementary school where it would become the core of the curriculum. I've often wished I were still in touch with him and could tell him about Philosophy for Children."

"How did you happen to hear about it?" I ask.

"Just before I went to China I attended a conference on critical thinking in Leningrad and, while there, I met a Professor Georg Brutian from Yerevan in Armenia—a specialist in argumentation. He mentioned it to me. Then, a bit later, in Moscow, I met a professor from the Department of Philosophy in Moscow State University. His name was Pokrovsky. He had been to the United States, had come across your program, and had said to himself, he told me, 'This is how philosophy ought to be written!'"

"And then you went to China."

"Yes, and it was at the offices of the *Guang Ming Daily* that I ran into a correspondent who had a friend in the Academy of Social Sciences. What this friend said was that they had already heard of you in China because the Academy had translated and published your book, *Contemporary Aesthetics*, and it had sold in the tens of thousands of copies. Then they received copies of your curriculum and they're beginning to translate that, too."

"Yes, but not the Academy. A private publisher is going to publish it. The translation is being done by the friend and his wife."

"Whatever. Anyhow, I became intrigued by the possibilities—and the rest I think I've already told you," she concludes.

"Natasha, when you—and Il'enkov and Vygotsky and their various progeny—when you all use the word 'philosophy,' what do you mean by it?"

"It's hard to say. It seems to me that the Western Europeans and the North Americans have one sense in mind and the Latin Americans have a second, we have a third, and in Asia, they have a fourth. But I'm not sure how these differences can be put into words. Will you help me? What is—for *you*—this thing called philosophy of which you have constructed a children's version?"

"Well, I guess I'd have to highlight two functions of philosophy," I reply. "One is analytical. Each discipline is reflective and, therefore, critical of its own knowledge. Philosophy involves the criticism of such criticism through an ongoing analysis of the criteria and standards employed."

"So if a child gives you a reason for something she said or did, that in itself need not be philosophy. But if she can supply a reason for thinking her first reason a good reason, her answer involves a philosophical inquiry?"

"Something like that. What we call art is taking the goods that nature provides us with and making other things that are just as good or better. What we call philosophy is an analysis of making and saying and doing, so that we can have criteria and standards that will permit us to say why some of these things are just as good or better than others."

"And the other function of philosophy?"

"The other function," I say, still groping my way, "is more synthesis than analysis, more speculative than empirical. To some extent, each philosopher tries, as Spinoza did, to construct a system of ideas with which everything that happens would be consistent."

"And to the extent that children form such frameworks of ideas so that what happens in their lives acquires its meaning in terms of such cognitive structures, to that extent they're being philosophical?"

"Unquestionably," I exclaim and then add, fearful of being too categorical, "I think so, anyhow. But what I don't have any doubt about is that children are marvelously speculative. Their minds are open because the barriers to such speculation have not yet been completely installed. And their minds are fertile and generative. Many adults develop ideas that they have secretly harbored since childhood—ideas that germinated in the early years of elementary school but lacked a suitable framework to lend them credibility. But we seldom give children credit for intellectual originality."

"I recall your writing somewhere about the dangers of 'pseudophilosophy,'" Natasha says softly. "Is it possible that the children in your program are just doing pseudophilosophy rather than genuine philosophical inquiry?"

"Yes, of course, just as many adults who claim to be doing professional philosophy may be simply going through a stock performance, an imitative routine, rather than engaging in what you refer to as 'genuine philosophical inquiry.' Look, the novels in my program are stuffed almost to bursting with genuine philosophical ideas derived from the tradition of academic philosophy, but detached from their historical settings. The instructional manuals are likewise stuffed with discussion plans that pose questions that come from a variety of philosophical perspectives and likewise are representative of the philosophical tradition. I cannot guarantee that children's responses to these philosophical provocations will be likewise philosophical, but that's not a theoretical matter, it's an empirical one."

"You mean all one has to do is listen to the dialogue of the children responding to such questions and one can tell at once whether that dialogue is philosophical or not?"

"I wish I could say that were the case," I answer. "But if teachers, for example, are not philosophically trained, they don't hear the philosophical dimension in the conversation of the children they teach. Conversely, many philosophers are so convinced that children cannot do philosophy that they won't acknowledge the philosophy in the conversation of such children, even when they overhear it."

"Are you saying, then, that the denial that children can do philosophy is largely a matter of a lack of open-mindedness on our part?"

"I think you can say that."

"Have you any explanation for such prejudice? Is it a prejudice to which psychology has lent support?"

"Yes—and here we come back to Vygotsky. To Vygotsky, a psychology that sought to explain the human in terms of the most rudimentary thought processes—on the excuse that these are the 'building blocks' of which the human being is comprised—has got its priorities turned upside-down. What we should be dealing with and attempting to explain is higher-order thought, not lower-order thought. I mean art and science and philosophy rather than eye-blinks and knee-jerks. But, because we have ignored Vygotsky's zone of proximal development, we have restricted our accounts of the child to his or her meanest competencies, rather than to those proficiencies he or she could develop—in art and science and philosophy—with adult assistance."

"Enough!" Natasha cries out. "On this point we don't disagree. But I'm beginning to get very conscious of time, and there are so many aspects of Davydov's approach that we haven't really given much attention to. Like his views on consciousness, on activity, on imagination and creativity, on discussion, on teaching, and on problem-solving. I know we can't deal with all of those, but would you mind very much if we touch on at least some of them before I have to call it quits? I'm beginning to get a number of other commitments and I've already spent much more time on this project than I'd planned. I so much enjoy thinking for its own sake, but I've also got to think to make a living. I just worry that my time is running out."

"Also known as," I remark, chronically unable to resist gilding the lily, "but thought's the slave of life and life's time's fool and time must have a stop." How pedantic can one get?

For my pains, I receive a wan smile of acknowledgment. Then she asks, "I wonder if I can ask you a favor. I need to do some research — it's sort of an emergency. Could you give me a letter of introduction to your college library so that I could use it for a few hours?"

In a few minutes the letter is written and signed and I tell her I'll walk part of the distance with her in order to show her the way. She asks to take another look at the peaceful little Greek amphitheater and I leave her to her reflections in front of the widening arcs of empty stone seats while I begin to retrace my steps toward College Hall. She must have stayed only a few moments because just as I reach the building, I hear a screech of brakes and the thud of impact. I spin around, lost in time, to see her tumbling across the roadway, her body coming to a halt only when it strikes the curb. A frightened student emerges from the car, a crowd gathers, the police and an ambulance arrive almost instantaneously, and Natasha is hurried off, unconscious, to Mountainside Hospital.

This stunning turn of events is only now beginning to sink in and I rush in my car to the hospital's emergency room, where I am told there is no information, so I will have to wait.

The minutes drag by like a queue of mourners saying their last goodbyes. I go over and over in my mind, cinematically, the sequence of events that I had glimpsed at the extreme periphery of my vision. With each imaginative rehearsal, what is borne in on me is the sheer, unrelieved superfluousness of the event, its totally dumb stupidity and meaninglessness.

Until this point, I have not allowed myself to think of consequences. All I have done is set up in my mind three formidable categories — fatally injured, injured but not critically, and relatively unharmed — and to try to fit the scenario I already know into one or another of these. But now I begin to wonder what will happen if . . . What will happen to her son and her stepfather if she is dead or injured? (She has told me that she is their sole support and that her only income is what she makes as a freelance translator in the encyclopedia division of a large publishing house.)

After several hours, a nurse arrives to tell me that the tests have been concluded and that her injuries are "not life-threatening." Half an hour later, a stumpy, bald doctor informs me that she has had a very close call but is relatively uninjured and is now conscious and can see me.

I thank him profusely and shake his hand, which he permits me to do. But he doesn't leave and, instead, scrutinizes me still more sharply and begins to ask about my relationship to her. At first I think maybe he is exceeding the bounds of justifiable professional inquisitiveness. I then wonder if perhaps his concern has to do with who will be responsible for the medical costs.

He assures me, however, that his attention has been attracted by something very different. "In the course of our examination," he explains, "we discovered that your friend has apparently gone without appropriate medical care for some time."

"Oh?" I say, bewildered.

"Yes," he says, scratching his cheek and his chin. "Her injuries are fairly minor: lots of bruises but no broken bones. But there's something else — a kind of profound exhaustion that she wishes to deny by insisting on her capacity for sustained hard work, all of which makes her still more exhausted."

"I can well imagine," I concur, recalling the many occasions on which she had insisted on struggling up the hill from the bus stop. "So you're saying she needs rest."

"Absolutely — several weeks of bed rest, at a minimum." And still he stands in front of me, as if debating with himself how much else to tell me. At last he remarks, "I should add that there are a number of other things that should be looked into. They may be symptomatic of something deeper, but we just don't know. I've told her that she needs a very thorough medical checkup and fairly soon. But more than that, I really can't tell you."

I ponder whether to reply, "You can't — or you don't want to?" But then I reason that this is Natasha's business, not mine.

"Good luck!" he says, as I proceed down the corridor of the ward toward her room.

She is a mass of bandages but alert and in fairly good spirits, considering what she has been through and the predicament she now finds herself in.

"Natasha," I say anxiously, "the doctor says you will need several weeks of bed rest —"

"Oh," she replies jauntily, "in a few days I'll be fine. All he means is that it will be a few days before I can take these bandages off and appear in public again."

I shake my head. "No, that's apparently not all he means. He told me that when they examined you they found a number of things that could be very serious."

An expression that I have seen before—of determination, or perhaps of plain stubbornness—now crosses her face. "We're never going to be homeless again," she mutters, half to herself. "I'll die first!"

I take my leave before our conversation, already in dire straits, takes another turn for the worse. Besides, I have the feeling she doesn't want me to meet her family, and they should be arriving fairly soon. As I depart, she calls out, "I'll give you a ring to let you know how I'm doing!"

I leave her to the harsh reality of her situation and traverse the hospital parking lot trying out predicates with which to characterize her behavior: "Upbeat? No. Indomitable? No. Tenacious? No . . . " Also, I marvel at what Grice would call the *implicature* of her linguistic move from the need for her getting a thorough medical examination to the possibility that this will lead to her becoming homeless. All the intervening steps are gone: the sobering diagnosis, the inability to work, the loss of income, the expulsion from the apartment. It is like a flight from one side of an abyss to the other. Then I think of what I am doing and I am ashamed. It is a morbid preoccupation; it is an affliction. Literary associations arise to fill the void: Merton Densher and Millie Theale in *The Wings of the Dove*; Philip Quarles and—was it Lucy Tantamount?— in *Point Counter Point* . . . I struggle to clear my head of these irrelevancies, these schematic, fictional scenarios that replace the real scenarios, the real schemata of our lives. It is clear that life's the slave of thought and time's life's fool and fools must have a stop . . .

SEVENTH VISIT

Two weeks go by, then a phone call comes and things attempt to resume where they left off. She is "grounded," as she quaintly puts it: must stay at home for at least some weeks. Would I consider visiting her and her stepfather, during which visit we can reconnect some of the loose strands of our previous conversations? Yes, of course I will. It is as if she has preempted the procedural part of inquiry, and without that, how can I proceed? I must struggle to get her to relinquish her hold over me. And part of that hold consists of my being sorry for her and her situation. Have I fallen victim to an informal fallacy — the appeal to pity? Perhaps. But I am determined to reassert my control over my own complex reasoning and not subcontract part of it to someone else.

On the bus into the city, I try to imagine what her stepfather will be like. Nothing in my movie experience will fit, so I try my image of Kandinsky on for size, but that doesn't fit either. Balanchine? No, definitely not. Igor Stravinsky? Now that's a possibility. I dwell on it all the way into the Port Authority Bus Terminal.

He turns out to be totally unlike Stravinsky but not totally unlike Nabokov — Vladimir, not the Russian composer Nicolas, although that, in turn, reminds me (to drop names once again) of a long conversation I had once had with Nicolas's attractive wife, a conversation that sounded very much to me like a call for help. But this is neither Nicolas nor Vladimir; rather it is a man intelligent and witty in his own right, although rather elderly now and perhaps in failing health. His glance is penetrating without being unfriendly and his manner is elegant without being affected. As I size him up, he is in the tradition of the cultivated European gentleman, as much at home in Florence, or Madrid, or Paris as in Leningrad or Moscow.

Natasha has been allowed out of bed for the occasion. She relaxes on the sofa now, in a voluminous velvet dressing robe. Avoiding small talk, she tries over and over again to steer the conversation back to Davydov. But her stepfather always manages to intercede in a gentle, unobjectionable way, and it is his curiosity rather than hers that tends to establish the agenda.

77

"My daughter has told me of your interest in Davydov," he remarks, sipping a glass of tea. He looks at me expectantly and I want to answer his question, but, at the same time, I am trying to take in the room, in which the magnificent samovar has established such a commanding presence. The wrought frames of the photographs and portraits, the graceful writing desk with a half-written letter on its open leaf, the decidedly continental knickknacks and bric-a-brac that fill the shelves, the porcelain and silver tea service, even the little wooden utility chest that he refers to affectionately as his "skopchik," or something like that. All of this breathes an atmosphere of the worldly Russian experience of the first quarter of this century, which is now so swiftly coming to an end — perhaps in more ways than one — a period that saw Kerensky and Trotsky and Lenin as well as the czar, that saw Pavlov as well as Vygotsky, futurism as well as impressionism, the Blue Rider group and *The Rite of Spring*, Mandelstam as well as Pasternak.

Bemused, I finally manage to say, "I'm really just barely acquainted with him. I've read two-thirds of his one book and, apparently, much of the theory is in the part I haven't yet read because it isn't yet translated. Of course, I'm also interested in Vygotsky — "

He chuckles. "No, no, that will never do! Pronounce it as if it were spelled Vy-*gut*-sky! Vy-*gut*-sky!"

Further abashed, I offer the comment that, for whatever reasons, Vygotsky himself had changed his name from the family spelling of Vygodsky — a spelling to which even his daughter, who is still alive and living in Moscow, has returned. "Why do you think he did that?" I ask.

Natasha's stepfather smiles faintly but mischievously. "Perhaps he didn't want 'god' to be a part of his name."

"Don't be ridiculous!" Natasha growls, speaking to her stepfather more boldly than I thought she would.

In defense of her stepfather, I comment, "We and our names have a most uncanny relationship, and I can well imagine a person changing his name in order to effect some magical change in himself."

Natasha demands, "And in this case, what could that be?"

"Well," I go on, accepting the tenuous path I seem to have been forced to follow, "Vygotsky — Vy-*gut*-sky — seemed to impress most people as downright charismatic — even Promethean. Maybe he wanted nothing to do with charisma; maybe he wanted a following based on reason rather than on faith. Maybe the person with 'god' in his name is in danger of thinking of himself as a god, and as Louis MacNeice says somewhere, 'Let not the man who thinks he is god come near me.'"

No one wants to pursue the matter any further: We prefer to let it die. After an appropriate moment of silence, Natasha's stepfather says to me, "You write philosophical books for children."

"Er—," I hesitate. "Put it this way: I write books that encourage children to do philosophy. I don't make it, or do it, or say it for them."

"That's very good! I like that!" he responds. "What led you to begin doing such a thing?"

Natasha groans. "The historical approach."

To her, I say, "Why not?" But to her stepfather, I counter with, "I've tried to answer that question a thousand times and each time I come up with a different answer. They're all true, and yet each is only a fragment of a truth that can never be fully established."

"Never?" Natasha inquires, skeptically.

"Never," I insist. "The experience can't happen again, and the documents that might attest to it or illuminate it are virtually nonexistent."

"Do you mean," says her stepfather, "that it was like what Buber calls a 'happening just once'?"

"Everything happens just once," I retort. "But some happenings are more 'just once' than others." He smiles appreciatively and Natasha frowns at my little joke.

He turns to Natasha. "You're unhappy that I am monopolizing the conversation with your guest. I'm sorry. I just want him to feel at home." He turns back to me. "Please call me Maxim, Matthew. And before you and Natasha go back to your Davydov, I'd just like to go back for a moment to what we were talking about before: What led you to writing these books."

Natasha murmurs, "Maxim, I really don't object to the topic. Anything you want to talk about is all right with me. We can get back to Davydov a little later. A little later, a little earlier, it doesn't matter. After all, my area of concern is with procedure, not with subject-matter." I notice that, in Maxim's presence, Natasha's accent is much more noticeable.

"So, Matthew!" Maxim says heartily, "Why philosophy in the form of novels? Why philosophy in the form of conversation?"

I grin. "Why philosophy in the form of children? All of these things make sense from one point of view and no sense at all from another. But to tell the truth, I can't help feeling quite embarrassed. My poor little stories are contrived to be springboards for philosophical dialogue, and they're terribly didactic. In no way are they comparable to real novels, which are designed to be read, not spoken or performed."

"Would you say that's true of *The Brothers Karamazov*?"

"Don't you see why I'm embarrassed?" I cry out. "As a philosophical novel, what can compare with *The Brothers Karamazov*?"

"You haven't answered my question. Is it designed only to be read?"

I stare at the samovar. "I read the *Karamazov* book aloud once, from cover to cover."

"And—?"

"It glowed—like a jewel in the dark."

Obviously pleased, Maxim gives me an encouraging glance and remarks, "Yes, it is a true philosophical novel, as opposed to genuine novels that contain philosophizing, like some of the novels of Mann and Tolstoy, or novels that are written from a specific philosophical point of view, like those of Sartre and Camus and de Beauvoir. Would you say your stories belong to either of those two types?"

I say, rather sheepishly, "No, they don't have a particular point of view and they don't contain much philosophizing. On the other hand, they have little character and less plot. I guess they're a different genre altogether."

"Like *The Little Prince*, perhaps?"

"No!" I exclaim. "*The Little Prince* is a masterful work. So is *Charlotte's Web*. But I think each of them emerges from a particular philosophical perspective and is designed to enchant us into acquiescing to that perspective, rather than to do philosophy ourselves."

"So yours are more like—let me think—more like, would you say, the works of Plato?"

I am beginning to see that behind Maxim's engaging exterior is a formidable interrogator. I resolve to be on my guard. The comparison with Plato is a trap for the unwary, just like the comparison with Dostoyevsky. "Sure," I say cautiously, "I used Plato's earlier works as a model. Sometimes I tried paraphrasing parts, the way Mickey in *Suki* paraphrases the last great speech by Thrasymachus in the *Republic*. Or sometimes I tried to interweave skill-building and concept-formation the way Socrates does in, say, the *Euthyphro*."

"So would you agree, then, that your works have no merit as literature?"

I hesitate before trying to answer this obviously loaded question. Finally, I say, "We tend to classify things in accordance with what they permit us to do with them. Take, for example, what English teachers consider literature. It consists of those works they can try to get their students to appreciate for their literary values. This is why English teachers seldom have a good word to say for Plato: His works don't lend themselves to literary appreciation or to literary criticism, for that matter. As I was saying to Natasha not long ago, English teachers will perhaps analyze the friendship between, say, Horatio and Hamlet, but seldom will they analyze the concept of friendship itself. To do so, to them, would be to move into the foreign territory of philosophy proper."

Natasha, scribbling furiously on her attaché case, nods vehement agreement.

Maxim adds, "Did you have any other models of philosophic dialogue besides Plato?"

"Very definitely—particularly Diderot's *Le Neveu de Rameau*, but also *Le Rêve de D'Alembert* and the *Supplément au Voyage de Bougainville*."

"And—even though you disclaim any literary ambitions—were there other literary models you had in mind?"

"Well, some of the *romans à clef* made me see the possibilities of treating ideas the way they treated people. Like, I mean, the novels of Aldous Huxley that I referred to a little while ago, or the novels of John Erskine—things like *The Private Life of Helen of Troy* or *Lancelot*—and some of D. H. Lawrence's novels."

"And what about the replacing of formal academic prose with casual conversation—what brought that on?"

"This replacement of the esoteric by the exoteric has been going on steadily since the Reformation began beating the drums for popular editions of the Bible. In the twentieth century, the welcoming of informality can be found everywhere, for example, in the way Bing Crosby and Fred Astaire succeed the formal singers and dancers of the first quarter of the century by means of an easy-going, conversational manner that enables them to dominate the next quarter of the century."

"So it's Bing Crosby and Fred Astaire, not the naturalness of Chekhov—?"

"Well," I respond quickly, "those were only examples. I could just as readily have mentioned William Carlos Williams or Montale. Or I could have referred to Bruner's dictum, that anything could be taught with integrity at any level, as legitimizing the translation of philosophy into the language of the young."

"Maxim," Natasha coos, "you've had him long enough now! It's *my* turn." Have we been discussing the absence of formality? Then I must mention its striking absence from the relationship here between stepfather and stepdaughter. They are more like two old friends. The suspicions aroused by Boris struggle to reassert themselves and I, for my part, struggle to expel them once and for all from my mind. I've no doubt that in Maxim's presence Natasha is a different person, but that might have been expected.

"So," I say, turning to face Natasha, "back to the future. Once more into Davydov, okay?" I spread some notes out on the coffee table in front of me.

"As you like," she says. "I seem to recall your saying you would like to take up his notion of *problem-solving*. Is that his term? I don't remember."

"He occasionally uses it, citing Bernshtein. Bernshtein says that animate bodies are future-oriented. They act rather than merely react. They explore and this 'living movement' can be called 'problem-solving' (Davydov, 1988a, 31). Davydov promptly remarks that 'living movement is the mind' (ibid., 32)."

"You find this sort of formulation congenial?" she asks.

"Well, it's familiar—let's put it that way. It's reminiscent of the pragmatists: Peirce, Mead, and, to some extent, Dewey. They argued that thinking arose out of blocked conduct. The organism might find that its usual way of coping with its environment wasn't working and it would feel frustrated. But then it might wonder if perhaps it was taking something for granted that shouldn't be taken for granted. Perhaps one of its unexamined beliefs or presuppositions was at fault and needed to be doubted. So it would try acting in ways not dictated by that belief. When the problem would be resolved, a new belief would replace the old one and conduct would be resumed."

"So thinking originates in doubting, but it also develops in the course of problem-solving, as we imaginatively test our hypothetical solutions."

"That sounds more like Dewey," I comment.

She laughs and, at the same time, twists about to get into a more comfortable position on the sofa. "Well, but it's also Gal'perin. He says that thinking is essential when we are faced with a unique rather than with an ordinary problem or task. In such cases, we can tackle the problem only if our action is preceded by testing in terms of images" (Davydov, 1988a, p. 33).

"Right, and Davydov cites Makhmutov's book, *Problem-Based Teaching*, on the same point. In fact, this is where Davydov offers a characterization of animal and human mind as 'the construction of images of objective reality and the exploration and testing of the basis of those images of movements and actions whose monitored performance leads to the satisfaction of perceived needs' (1988a, p. 33). Do we need to spend any more time on this point?"

"No, let's go on."

"Okay. Now Davydov takes as axiomatic Vygotsky's dictum that teaching precedes, shapes, and stimulates the child's mental development. This leads Davydov to develop the notion of teaching as 'formative experimentation,' which bears some resemblance to Dewey's characterization of his own philosophy as experimentalism."

Natasha nods. "The formative experiment, as I remember his lecture on it, involves the teacher's doing research at the same time as doing teaching. The teacher/researcher actively intervenes in the mental processes of the children under study and brings about new mental formations through that intervention (Davydov, 1988d). Davydov calls it 'an experiment in genesis-modeling' (ibid., p. 53), and Vygotsky refers to it as 'the application of the causal-genetic method' (quoted ibid., p. 52). The aim is to move the children to new levels of ability development while, at the same time, studying the regularities of mental development in the forward movement."

"Did you have a role in Davydov's research into the formative experiment?"

Maxim interjects, "She certainly did —," but Natasha gives him a steely glance and his voice trails off.

Natasha throws her head back just a bit and explains, "I was a member of the research team that was under the general supervision of El'konin and Davydov. The project was headquartered in Moscow's School #91 as well as in Kharkov. I was in the Kharkov branch and I taught in the younger grades — first through third. Some of the other teachers taught in grades 4 through 8."

"So as a researcher/teacher, you conducted formative experiments in order to see if Vygotsky's theory regarding the role of teaching in development could be verified?"

"Yes. The actual project lasted for 25 years — from 1959 to 1984" (Davydov, 1988d, pp. 54–55).

"And the experimental results?"

"They were excellent. The experimental groups significantly outperformed the comparison groups, even in the teaching of art" (Davydov, 1988e, p. 15). Once again, there is that peculiar little toss of the head as Natasha adds, "There is no period of my life of which I am more proud than the years I spent in that research work. But enough of that. What other aspects of problem-solving would you still like to review?"

"Just a few," I reply. "For example, there's planning. The teacher/researcher evidently helps children formulate plans of action."

"That is correct. Davydov thinks there's a direct correlation between the mastery of children's planning and the mastery of their execution and expression (1988e, p. 14)." With a note of irritation, she adds, "What are you laughing at?"

"At the fact that, although we may not be doing reciprocal teaching, we *are* certainly doing reciprocal inquiry!" I am solemn again.

"Please!" she begs. "I'm getting very tired. Can we finish this topic?"

"Well," I say, "planning leads to something Davydov calls modeling, but I'm not sure what he means by that. He claims that at the heart of the object of investigation — what I suppose we would call the subject-matter of inquiry — is a general relationship that can be expressed in an appropriate theoretical concept (1988c, p. 31). The students in the learning process are encouraged to try to express this universal relationship, either graphically or literally. This is what is meant by *modeling*, apparently. Still concentrating on the relationship, the students are encouraged to engage in transformations of the model (ibid.). Can you make some sense of this for me?"

"I don't see that it's all that difficult or obscure," she replies. "The teacher sets a task — "

I interrupt: "The children don't find the problem for themselves?"

"Maybe they do, maybe they don't," Natasha snaps. "But in any case, the teacher encourages them to do their own planning. It's just that the teacher sets certain task conditions that the students are expected to conform to."

"I'm confused. Could you give me an example?"

"Of course. Suppose it's an art class. The teacher may say, 'Now, the task conditions are that something is to be in motion and something else is to be motionless'" (Davydov, 1988e, p. 12).

"Oh," I exclaim, "I like that! So the initial requirements involve a major conceptual opposition, like in pre-Socratic philosophy: permanence versus change, motion versus rest, the eternal versus the temporal, and so on! These are the sorts of conceptual puzzles we involve children in when they read *Kio and Gus*! And they're the sort of binary criteria I talk about when I discuss creative thinking in *Thinking in Education*!"

Natasha seems amused at my outburst. "Let me go on," she says firmly, after having momentarily lost the page she was looking at. "The students make their plans by means of cut pieces of paper, dark right-angled shapes that they divide into moving and stationary. (Those who are onlookers have to try to tell which is which. They also try to guess the contents of the pictures from the arrangements of the shapes.) The children debate these guesses. They are rearranging the shapes to find out, if they can, the best way of conveying the plan of each picture" (Davydov, 1988e, pp. 12-13).

"Yes," I say quickly, "now I remember it! This is where the students have to play the roles of artist and viewer, and then they have to exchange roles with one another. In so doing, they are *monitoring* the creative process" (ibid., p. 13).

"Precisely," Natasha concurs. "As Davydov puts it somewhere — here it is — 'Monitoring consists in determining the correspondence between other learning actions and the conditions and requirements of this particular learning task' (1988c). For example, the students may learn how to make a certain measurement, involving a series of operations. Then the teacher changes one of the operations — say, by doing it incorrectly. If the students are monitoring their work effectively they will be able to understand why the results, this time, are different and what has to be done to correct the measurement" (Davydov, 1988d, p. 33).

I can see that Natasha is now quite fatigued and when I say that I must go, Maxim throws me an appreciative glance that suggests he had been hoping for some time I would make such a move.

On the bus back from New York, the question reasserts itself in my mind of what it must mean to Davydov that "a system of particular tasks be constructed that can be resolved by a general mode" (1988c, pp. 31–32). The glimmer of comprehension I begin to get derives from my using the Philosophy for Children manual as an analogy. In the manual, we first identify a concept (for instance, friendship) and then we provide exercises and discussion plans that concretize the concept by considering various possible manifestations of it. Before I know it, I'm at the bus stop for the college, humming a theme from *La Traviata* that has somehow gotten lodged in my head.

EIGHTH VISIT

As I had no word from Natasha the following week, I call. Maxim answers and says that Natasha's condition has worsened somewhat, so that he has persuaded her to go to the hospital for a few days. He gives me no clue as to what sort of illness she has.

When I tell Teri about this, she suggests that I send Natasha a get-well card, and then adds, "By the way, did you ever resolve all those questions that Boris raised about Natasha?"

"Oh, yes," I reply quickly, "all of them. And Boris agrees he was mistaken. He confused Natasha with her mother, who really did work for the NKVD, or OGPU, or whatever it was called in those days."

Teri frowns. "One thing I recall still troubles me. I mean, about her father being killed at Smolensk. But the war ended in 1945, so that would make Natasha at least 45 years old. Yet you told me she was in her 30s."

I agree. "I'll call Boris," I say.

Teri sniffs. "I wonder when you'll learn that your friend Boris is not exactly a model of reliability."

I call Boris anyhow, and he assures me once again that he was completely mistaken about Natasha and that all his accusations against her were invalid.

"What about her father being killed at Smolensk? That would make her at least 45 years old!"

"No, not at all," Boris says soothingly. "He wasn't killed in the war. He was killed in an airplane accident — at Smolensk — in 1971."

I hang up and tell Teri what Boris said. "So see!" I say triumphantly, "It was all just a case of mistaken identity."

Teri gives me a skeptical glance but says nothing.

I call several times over the next few weeks, but Maxim is very uninformative, except to say that Natasha is still taking tests in the hospital.

But then one day I call and Natasha herself answers the phone. She sounds almost cheerful. "Yes," she says, "I'm back. We need to finish our project. I'm afraid I'm still not up to traveling. Could you come here?"

Their apartment, in the West 90s, is in a rather run-down brownstone. It's on the third floor — a "railroad" apartment with a long, dark hall, rooms with closed doors off to either side, opening into a spacious, high-ceilinged living room. (Somehow, the first time I was there, the living room was the only part of the apartment that registered on me.)

Maxim brings some coffee and croissants, and I relax in the same deep, comfortable armchair I had occupied on the last visit. But Natasha is not one to waste time. "I have been talking to Boris," she announces, to my astonishment.

All I can say is "Oh?"

"He tells me he made some accusations against me."

"Yes, he did, but that's all been resolved. There's really no need to talk about these things, and I'm sure it's not very pleasant for you." I don't know where Natasha is taking the conversation, and I'm apprehensive.

She drops her head for a moment, then raises it and looks at me directly. "You must know."

"I must know what?"

"My mother worked for them. That's true. She wasn't forced to. She did it because she believed in it."

I am silent. I glance for a moment at Maxim, but his face tells me nothing.

Natasha continues, "They kept an eye on me. They knew I spoke English and Chinese well and could be useful to them, but they left me alone. Then I met Mikhail, and before I knew it, I was carrying Sergei. When Mikhail told me he couldn't marry me, I became frantic. I told myself I couldn't stay in the same country with him. But I had no money, and Maxim had already gone to the United States. As my situation deteriorated, I became desperate. I went to the government and asked if I could get a job in the United States, in the Soviet embassy, as a translator. They told me no, but that they had a counteroffer. It would mean working in China. I won't tell you what it involved, but all I could say to myself was, 'Like mother, like daughter.'"

"So Boris was actually right!" I exclaim. "I feel like I'm on a rollercoaster!"

"I can assure you," Natasha says, "I had the same feeling. Every day I did dangerous things, perilous things."

"While carrying Sergei?"

"While carrying Sergei. It was a relief finally when he arrived, and I was permitted to look for other work. That's when I became a Soviet correspondent in Beijing, although I can assure you that, for a long time, I had to do much more than file newspaper articles."

"And subsequently?" I ask.

"I've nothing new to tell you about what happened subsequently. To tell the truth — " she pauses to smile and finish her coffee, "I feel very good about being able to tell the truth."

"Good enough!" I say. "And now, shall we get back to Davydov?"

Natasha doesn't exactly look thrilled by the prospect. "I know there are many other facets of his work we haven't yet touched on, but Maxim is dying to bring up another topic, and I'm wondering if we can't let Davydov alone for now."

"It's all right with me," I respond. "Maxim?"

Maxim seems to have been lost in thought, but when I call out his name, he looks startled. "Yes, absolutely, I do have a question for you. I want to know whether, before you wrote your novels for children, you had read Bakhtin."

"No," I say, "not at all. Why do you ask?"

"I'm interested in the *voice* you adopt, as the voice of the narrator."

"Actually," I point out, "the first four books to have been written are for children from 11 to 17, and they are the only ones that have a narrator. The other three, for younger children, are written in the first person. And even in the case of the first four books, the narrator doesn't play a very large role."

"Yes," Maxim says. "When I read *Harry* for the first time, I thought the narrator might just possibly be a child of Harry's age."

"Even in *Harry*, I was trying to get away from the authoritative narrator's voice and the authoritative narrator's point of view," I say. "Children find that voice intimidating. When they hear it, they no longer feel free to think for themselves. I'm reminded of those experiments the cognitive scientist Jill de Villiers conducted at MIT, in the 1980s, I believe, with children of kindergarten age. At first they were exposed to an adult who made many grammatical mistakes in speaking with them. But the children seemed not to notice the mistakes. The children were then presented with a delightful talking doll that was wired with a secret microphone. When the doll talked, its conversation was also full of grammatical errors. But now the children pointed out to the doll his mistakes, as well as the grammatical rules that he was violating. Now *they* were the authorities."

Natasha asks, "What do the teachers of English language and literature have to say about your books?"

"Well, some of them try to be kind and say that their students don't like the books: They find them boring. Then the teachers will add something like, 'and they *are*, of course, *quite* badly written.'"

Natasha asks, "Does that bother you?"

"Well, they think their primary task is to get children to *appreciate* the best literature there is, and so they don't take kindly to poor models. When I ask if they would like their students to learn to read *critically*, they look very pained."

"Of course!" Natasha says emphatically. "What good is it to be able to read critically, if you can't appreciate the values of what you're reading? Both skills are necessary."

With a faint smile, Maxim returns to his Bakhtin agenda. "So your books for younger students are solely dialogue and no narration, in order to avoid what Wertsch, following Bakhtin, calls 'the voice of decontextualized rationality'?"

"Certainly," I agree. "That's the voice in which objects and events are represented in terms of formal, logical, and even quantifiable categories. These categories are decontextualized: Their meaning is derived from their position in abstract theories that are independent of particular speech contexts. For example, the meaning of *five* is independent of particular use and is identical across various contexts."

Natasha laughs: "It's the voice some men put on — the cold, authoritative, critical voice, the voice of logic and pure reason!"

I realize that I'm being twitted, and I can't help responding in kind: "And don't some women put on the contrasting voice of contextualized representation, the voice that issues from their personal identity and from the concrete situations in which they find themselves?"

Maxim protests, "You're treating these two voices as caricatures!"

"Not really," I say in rejoinder, "because I think they're 'ideal-types' that help us understanding thinking. I mean, much of our thinking is a dialogue between these two voices. Maybe that's too strong. Maybe I should limit the dialogue to our deliberations, where we're trying to arrive at a judgment. It's in such cases that we weigh what is said through contextualized forms of expression as over against what is said through the voice of decontextualized rationality."

"So," says Maxim, "what you're telling me is that, in thinking, there is a dialectical confrontation between these two voices — the decontextualized voice and the contextualized voice. And this opposition of thesis and antithesis is surmounted by, what would you call it, 'rational dialogue'?"

"I'm not saying that always happens," I respond quickly. "Many times it doesn't. Maybe most times it doesn't. But the novels are constructed so as to present a model of reasonable dialogue as the product of the interplay between those two voices. As I've said before, children need models of how to think: It's not enough just to sharpen their reasoning skills."

Natasha asks, "Isn't the voice of decontextualized authority the result of internalization, and doesn't that show a connection with Vygotsky?"

"As far as we know," says Maxim, "Bakhtin and Vygotsky never met."

"But they could have both been influenced by Weber," I point out. "Weber's thesis that the Reformation represented the internalization of external authority was well known throughout Europe, including Russia, shortly after it came out, in 1904 or 1905 — somewhere around that time. It seems to me very likely that Weber was the source of Vygotsky's idea of internalization."

"And where might Weber have gotten it?" Maxim asks. "Have you any idea?"

"Possibly from Simmel. I don't know. It's a long time since I wrote anything about Simmel, but it seems to me that it might have touched on this question. The first part of Weber's essay, *The Protestant Ethic and the Spirit of Capitalism*, appeared three or four years before Simmel's *Sociology* was published, but Weber was already familiar with Simmel's ideas. In fact, the key notion of reciprocity, which we — Natasha and I — talked about on our very first meeting, seems to have been first developed systematically by Simmel and then picked up and formalized by Weber. In the second quarter of the twentieth century, when the activities of Vygotsky and Bakhtin were at their height, the idea of reciprocity was to be examined assiduously by anthropologists and sociologists like Malinowski, Lévi-Strauss, and Talcott Parsons, while the theme of internalization was being examined by Mead and Piaget."

Maxim smiled. "I'm surprised you make no mention of Durkheim."

"You're absolutely right — my omission. Durkheim developed the notion of the internalization of external authority in the late 1890s, almost at the same time (1893) that Simmel was exploring it in his much more microscopic way. Anyhow, I was just trying to put Vygotsky into some kind of historical framework, so as to show how he took ideas that were very much 'in the air' in his day, gave them a decisive twist, and set them off in a wholly new direction."

Maxim offers me more coffee but I wave it off. He pours some for Natasha, but without asking. As he does so, he asks, "So, now, why are you interested in Davydov? Is it because you think he has made significant contributions to Vygotsky's zone of proximal development?"

"On the contrary," I say, with some warmth, "I'm no longer sure he has contributed a great deal in that particular area. The concept of the ZPD has been hailed as Vygotsky's greatest achievement, but people like the cognitive psychologist Jonathan Tudge are now beginning to discover some of its limitations. And some people are beginning to say that the concept may have made an important contribution to the theoretical literature, but it was always understood and utilized in *practice*. Maybe this is why Davydov seems to have backed off from it somewhat."

"Da," says Maxim, with a little chuckle, "so I repeat: Why Davydov now?"

"Well, to answer that question, I have to be up front with you not only with regard to my reasons, but also with regard to my motives. As for the former, it's no secret that my primary reason or purpose is to make philosophy available to children —"

"For the good of philosophy?"

"No — or at least, not primarily, but for the good of the children themselves. I am absolutely convinced of that. Second, I now think Davydov's major theme is the ascent from the abstract to the concrete. And third, it is this concept that I see providing a theoretical haven or enclosure for Philosophy for Children. Not the whole of that enclosure, of course, but a vital part of it."

"So you're saying that it is not enough for you to have produced a redesigned version of philosophy that you claim to be suitable for children. Nor is it enough to show that it works in the classroom — that children enjoy it and that it improves their education significantly. What you seem to be saying is that the educators and educational psychologists who are the arbiters and custodians of school programs — or at least of the criteria by means of which such programs are accepted or rejected on theoretical grounds — are dead set against your program because it runs counter to their establishment conceptions of what education is all about, is that right?"

"Yes, I can only invoke a minority, dissenting voice among them — the voice of Vygotsky and his followers, most notably Davydov. But even these do not necessarily recognize the match or correspondence between what they say they want and what we have to offer them."

Maxim shakes his head slowly from side to side. "I'm afraid half the people consider any educational program of any value or integrity a worthless panacea, and the other half consider every worthless panacea a promise of educational excellence. They are uncritical; they lack standards; they cannot make the necessary judgments."

"I'm not so sure of that," I reply. "But I do want to reassure people that philosophy in the elementary school is not a misbegotten monstrosity: It fits into educational, philosophical, and psychological traditions, although not necessarily the most familiar ones. It has theoretical sanction as well as empirical backing. This is why I want to spell out those traditions and invoke them or appeal to them."

Maxim laughs and slaps his knee. "Good luck! Weber and Simmel are just as much anomalies today in sociology as Vygotsky is in psychology! Sure, if they were everywhere accepted, you could appeal to them and show that your approach is more consistent with aspects of theirs than is the accepted approach in education. But to this day, they remain outsiders, and so, I think, will you, for a long time to come."

Natasha, who has not been taking notes for a while, but who has been resting her head on the back of the sofa, with her eyes closed, now rouses herself to interject, "Maxim!"

"I'm sorry," Maxim says, genuinely apologetic. "But let's go back a bit. You seem to be saying that there are various strands of tradition in scholarship and that each generation puts forward new performers to express each strand. Thus you see Davydov's performance as being in the Vygotskean tradition just as much as, say, Prokofiev's composition is a performance in the classical tradition." When I nod, he continues, "And who is in the tradition of, say, G. H. Mead?"

"I would say someone like C. Wright Mills, although there are many more recent advocates of Mead's position, as interactional social psychology or as transactional sociology."

"And is there a contemporary representative of Dewey's position in education?"

"There are numerous claimants, but I have the *hubris* to say that Philosophy for Children is the only valid representative of Dewey's educational ideas put into practice."

At this, Natasha opens her eyes. "Please," she appeals, "I must protest against the way you caricature your own position! You are making it sound to Maxim as if your curriculum contains nothing but Deweyan ideas put into the mouths of infants. Why do you talk this way? I've even heard it said that the objective of your Philosophy for Children is to indoctrinate children with your personal philosophy! Can you imagine!"

I hasten to agree, "No, no, Natasha, you're perfectly right. The curriculum has to be representative of the entire tradition of academic philosophy, just as an encyclopedia of philosophy has to represent every philosopher, every movement, and every school fairly and dispassionately. As editor of the curriculum, I try to be impartial, so that every point of view gets a hearing, if I can be permitted to mix my metaphors a bit."

Accepting my little joke with a pained smile, Maxim inquires, "Are we coming back to the notion of 'point of view' so that we can discuss it for a bit? I'd like to. I mean, it appears to be of cardinal importance in Mead's theory, but Wertsch seems to be putting it in the same class as 'roles,' which for him are Mead's concepts, and which Wertsch feels are abstract and analytic, in contrast with Bakhtin's more concrete forms of analysis."

"That's fine with me!" I respond. "Look, there's no disagreement between Mead and Bakhtin on this point, although one looks at points of view abstractly and developmentally while the other looks at them in their particularity. The important question that this approach sheds light on is the epistemological question as to the role of perspectives in arriving at objective knowledge."

"Oh, please!" Natasha wails.

"All right! All right!" I tell her. "Let me just say this. Take that body of knowledge called philosophy. It is constituted of many expressions, each drawn from distinctively different points of view, and its objectivity lies in their totality. Now, elementary school philosophy is comprised of a variety of expressions, each of which is a counterpart of the differently nuanced expressions of academic philosophy. Don't you see, they have a one-to-one correspondence."

Natasha shakes her head. "No," she says, "it's a one-to-many correspondence." Amused at my puzzled look, she continues, picking up a copy of *Harry* that has been lying, along with the other children's novels, on the coffee table in front of the sofa. "See, I choose a passage — not altogether at random — and I read it to you. It's from Chapter 17, the final chapter."

"It seems to me," said Fran, "that Tony and Lisa could both be right. I don't know quite how to say this because I haven't thought of it before. But I've been thinking, while I've been sitting here listening — I've been thinking of how all of us are here in one room. And it's the same room for all of us. And yet —" Fran stopped. "Oh, I don't know."

"Go on, Fran," Mr. Spence said gently, "what is it you started to say?"

"I can't seem to express it," said Fran. "But you know, here I am, sitting in the back of the room, and you're up there at the front of the room. And what do you see? You see faces. And what do I see? I see the backs of people's heads."

"And I'm sitting on the side of the room," exclaimed Anne, "and I see everyone from the side. I see their faces in profile."

"Well, that's what I mean," said Fran. "We're looking at exactly the same people in exactly the same room, and yet what we actually see is altogether different."

"So what you're saying," said Anne, "is that each of us is in the same world, yet we see things very differently. Oh, I know that's so true, because when Laura and I go to art class together, and even when we choose exactly the same still life to do, her paintings come out very different from mine. I think Fran's right. I think each of us lives in his own world that's different from other people's."

Now Harry was waving his hand wildly. Mr. Spence nodded at him.

"Anne," said Harry, "I think you didn't interpret Fran correctly. I mean, I don't think that's what she was trying to say. Sure, from the back of the room, she sees a roomful of people with their backs turned to her, while Mr. Spence sees only faces. But the important point is that, if she were to go up front, she would see only faces, and if Mr. Spence were to go to the back of the room, he would see only backs of heads."

"Harry," said Lisa, "is all you're trying to say that we should try to see things from other people's points of view?"

"I guess so," said Harry.

"Well," exclaimed Lisa, her eyes sparkling, "why doesn't anyone here try to understand my point of view? I disagree with you, and right away everyone accuses me of copping out on the class, or of being a fink, or something like that."

"Lisa," said Mr. Spence, "I don't think anyone here called you names or accused you of copping out. The trouble is, you've never really explained to us what you were objecting to. I wish you'd try to do so, just one more time. We'd like to be able to see things from your point of view, Lisa, but you haven't yet told us what it is."

"I don't think I can, Mr. Spence," Lisa said, trying to keep her voice steady, but not quite succeeding.

"I see what you're trying to get me to do," I say, when Natasha has completed her dramatically expressive reading of the passage. "You want me to show you a theoretical counterpart of this that you've just read. Well—" here I fish around among my notes until I come up with this passage from *The Sociology of Georg Simmel*:

If A and B have different conceptions of M, this by no means necessarily implies incompleteness or deception. Rather, in view of the relation in which A stands to M, A's nature and the total circumstances being what they are, A's picture of M is true for him in the same manner in which, for B, a different picture is true. It would be quite erroneous to say that, above these two pictures, there is the objectively correct knowledge about M, and that A's and B's images are legitimated to the extent to which they coincide with this objective knowledge. Rather, the ideal truth which the picture of M is in the conception of A approaches—to be sure, only asymptotically—is something different, even as an ideal, from that of B. It contains as an integrating, form-giving precondition that psychological peculiarity of A and the particular relation into which A and M are brought by their specific characters and destinies. (Simmel, trans. 1964, p. 309)

"Now," I say, "isn't that the sort of thing you mean?"

Natasha gives me a somewhat exasperated look. "It's the *sort* of thing I mean, of course! And that's just my point. But on the one hand, there are many passages in the literature that have a correspondence with what I read you from *Harry*, and not just your Simmel passage. So that's what I meant by a 'one-to-many' correspondence. On the other hand, what Simmel is saying in the passage you read, although it resembles the *Harry* passage in some ways, is different from it in many other ways."

Maxim massages his chin and remarks, in a musing tone, "But then, aren't you guilty of indoctrinating children with the idea of objectivity?"

"I don't see how," I reply quickly. "So long as the inquiry is merely going where it leads and can go off in a different direction tomorrow, so long as there is an abundance of skeptics in the class, like Lisa, for example, then I see no harm in taking up ideas at one point and putting them down at another—after having examined them—so long as that is what the inquiry calls for and what we choose to do."

"But you personally, apart from your curriculum," says Maxim softly, "aren't you advocating relativism?"

"I see four positions on the table," I reply. "Absolutism, relativism, objectivism, and subjectivism. I do not advocate the first and the fourth. As for the second and third, I think I would advocate them conjoined—as 'objective relativism.' Of course, in saying this, I am merely echoing Buchler."

"Do you always keep track of the sources of your ideas?" Natasha asks.

"Well, that's a relationship, and I try to keep track of my relationships. Doesn't everyone?"

Natasha and Maxim both laugh and exclaim, simultaneously, "No!"

As I continue to expound on the difference between the nonpartisan character of the curriculum and the partisan views I may happen to have as a particular individual, I notice Maxim getting restless, and he notices that I notice. "Continue, my friend," he says. "It's time for me to get Sergei from school. It's only a block from here; I'll be right back."

When Maxim leaves, Natasha says to me, "I don't know what I'd do without him."

"Without — Sergei?"

Natasha smiles. "No — I was speaking of Maxim. He has literally saved my life. There are so many ways in which I am indebted to him, and yet he asks nothing of me except to be allowed to help take care of Sergei." What she says is disarming and constructive. Even so, I have the feeling that she is choosing her words with care and is observing me closely as she speaks.

She continues to relate the many ways Maxim has of being helpful. Then, in only a matter of minutes, he is back with Sergei, who throws his arms around his mother's neck and is given a great hug in return.

"Well, Sasha," she says, "how did school go this morning?"

"All right," he says. "Who's this?"

Natasha reddens, "Oh, I'm sorry! I forget to introduce you!" She quickly explains the reason for my visit.

"Sasha," says Maxim, "you still haven't answered your mother's question: How did school go today?"

Sergei answers lightly, "Okay, I guess." He balances a book on his head.

"Anything interesting happen?"

Again the nonchalant tone: "No." The book falls off and he squeals with laughter.

"Have you had anything to eat?" Natasha asks.

"We had a snack."

"What did you have?"

"We had plums." At this point, Sergei seems to remember something and his face lights up. His words tumble over each other: "Mrs. Apel — Mrs. Apel, she — Mrs. Apel gave us plums!"

Natasha exclaims, "She did! Oh, that must have been nice!"

"Yes," Sergei says. The book is now balanced again on his head. "First she showed us a plum, and she said, 'What is this?' and we said, 'A plum!' She asked us, 'When you look at it, do you see the word *plum*?' and we said 'No!' Then she hid the plum in her desk and wrote the word *plum* on the board: *p-l-u-m*. And she asked us, 'When you look at the word, do you see the plum?' and we said, 'No!'"

Maxim, Natasha, and I exchange glances. The book falls to the floor and Sergei now attempts to stand on his head, using the book as a cushion. Natasha asks him, "What's the relationship between the plum and the word *plum*?"

Sergei's voice is a bit muffled, as he tries to talk upside-down: "It's like — it's like — it's like the way the pit of the plum is to the part you eat."

"I don't understand," says Natasha.

Sergei stretches out face down on the floor. "Can I go to my room now? I want to read my book."

Natasha tosses her head in the direction of his room, and Sergei scampers away instantaneously. "What's he talking about?" she asks me.

"My guess is —" I say, "I think what he's getting at is that, just as the pit of the plum is surrounded by the edible part, so the plum itself is surrounded by the sphere of the word — the sphere of knowledge."

Natasha turns to Maxim. "Is that how you see it, too?"

"Much the same," Maxim remarks. "It's as though everything concrete has an abstract envelope. We can experience things themselves, but we can understand them only by getting to know the envelopes that enclose them."

"I had just about the same interpretation," says Natasha. "But I would have put it in terms of particulars and universals. We can touch and taste and smell a particular plum. But to know what plums are, we have to employ universals, like the word *plum*."

"In what sense do you use the word *universal*?" Maxim inquires.

"In two senses, I guess," Natasha replies. "The word *plum* is universal in the sense that it applies to all plums. And second, it's universal in the sense that its references to all plums is understood by all human beings."

"I have no objection to that," I comment, "but I'd like to go back to the concrete–abstract distinction we were talking about a moment ago. I would say that there are four concentric spheres in this illustration. There is first the pit of the plum, where the pit represents the plum in its utter particularity, its dumb, arcane, inedible heart. Then there's the second sphere, that of the delicious flesh of the plum, and the third, the rich, purple skin of the plum. All these are particular and concrete. Finally comes the fourth concentric sphere, the sphere of knowledge-about-plums, the sphere of putting into words what it's like to be a plum, the sphere of utter abstraction." I glance at my watch. "But I'm afraid I can't stay here uttering abstractions, much as I enjoy doing so. I've got to run." As I say it, I recall those occasions when Natasha would suddenly rise and be off to the bus stop.

"So long," I say to Maxim, and I reach out my hand to him. Just as I do, an association leaps to mind, and I mutter, half-aloud, "Mead."

"I'm sorry, I didn't catch what you said," Maxim remarks.

"It was nothing," I reply.

"Was it — did it have something to do with George Herbert Mead?"

"As a matter of fact, yes, I take it you are familiar with Mead?"

"I remember Bruner mentioning him in the introduction to Vygotsky's *Thought and Language*. I gathered that he didn't think much of the comparison of Mead with Vygotsky. In any case, I've tried reading Mead, but haven't gotten very far."

"Well," I answer, "I think that, for each of the key Vygotskean phrases we've mentioned — like 'from the abstract to the concrete' or 'from the interpsychical to the intrapsychical' — there's an exposition by Mead that corresponds roughly to the expositions by Vygotsky and Davydov. What's more, there are huge areas where Vygotsky is relatively silent but where Mead is quite articulate. It is in these areas that Mead complements Vygotsky. But look, I must go." And I move down the long, dark hallway toward the door.

Natasha waves good-bye and goes off in the direction of Sergei's room. Maxim accompanies me to the door. As we stand under the light in the dingy corridor, I can see the lines of care in his face and the troubled shadows in his eyes. If there is something he would like to tell me, he cannot bring himself to say it, but I have no doubt that it has to do with Natasha. Silently he shakes his head and his eyes glisten.

NINTH VISIT

Several weeks go by. There is no answer when I call and no messages arrive from either Maxim or Natasha. Then the phone rings, and it is her unmistakable voice. (I say unmistakable because I've been trying to pinpoint what makes it so different. I think now I have it: Unlike most people, she neither aspires to perfect pitch when she speaks nor does she speak off-key. Rather, it's as though her voice floats around each note, the way a butterfly flutters close to and then away from a flower.) I have gotten lost in reflection momentarily and have to rouse myself to attend to what she is asking.

"Is there a preschool on your campus?"

"Yes, I think so," I answer. "Do you want me to find out?"

"Please. And call me back."

I call her back to tell her there is. "Good!" she exclaims. "Maxim has bought a car and he will drive us to your campus."

"He'll stay in the nursery while we talk about George Herbert Mead? I can't imagine he'll be very happy with that arrangement."

Natasha giggles. "No, don't be silly! Maxim will come with us!"

When they arrive, we all walk over to the drop-in center where the nursery is located. Sergei takes to it immediately, and so the three of us move on to the cafeteria in the student center.

To my surprise, Natasha takes a hearty breakfast. When she is absent for a moment, I glance inquisitively at Maxim. In a low, husky voice he says, "She's in remission." If, when she returns, she thinks we might have been talking about her, she gives no sign of it.

"So," she says, getting out her notepad at last, "what is it that Mead says that Vygotsky says?"

"And what is it that Mead says that Vygotsky doesn't say?" Maxim adds.

"Come on, now," I protest, "I can't make a point-by-point comparison of the two of them, especially since my knowledge of both of them is pretty skimpy. Look, let me just take up a few points — "

"Like the ascent from the abstract to the concrete and from the interpsychical to the intrapsychical — just as you promised," Natasha says. "A promise is a promise is a promise."

"Oh," I exclaim, "did I ever tell you about my meeting with Gertrude Stein? It was just after the war on Christmas Eve in the old Hotel Republique in Paris—"

"Professor—" Natasha growls.

"Okay, okay," I tell her. "Look, Piaget says we shouldn't push abstractions on children until they're ready—unaided—to handle them. Vygotsky says children need abstract knowledge to complement their concrete acquaintance with the world and we should let adults (and sometimes peers) help them acquire that abstract understanding. Now Mead isn't speaking pedagogically, but he *is* arguing, nevertheless, that abstract thought is indispensable, not only for the child's continuing education but also for the child's becoming a self or, as we would nowadays more likely put it, a person."

I stop while Natasha scribbles. Without looking up, she rumbles, "Keep going!"

"Natasha!" I say. "Do you remember how it was when Sergei was still an infant and you were feeding him with a spoon? When you would offer him a spoonful of food, what would you do at the same time?"

"I'd open my mouth," she says with a little laugh. "I couldn't help doing it. I guess it's instinctive."

"Well, Mead wouldn't classify it as instinctive at all. He'd call it a social response."

"A response to what?"

"To your offering Sergei a spoonful of food. Both you and he would respond to *your* offer in the same way, which insured that what *you* did had the same meaning for *both* of you."

"Because the meaning of an act consists of the consequences it evokes?"

"Right. The old pragmatic principle."

"Give us another example," Natasha asks.

"Okay. You think a strange man has winked at you flirtatiously. But in reality it is only a nervous tic. Since his gesture does not mean to him what it seems to mean to you, there has been no communication."

Maxim looks skeptical. He shrugs and looks at Natasha with his hands outstretched, palms up. But then he asks, "What I'm trying to get you to tell me is where Vygotsky and Mead see eye to eye. For example, what about consciousness—do they have similar views on that?"

"Well," I reply, "they both protest that they're not very much interested in plain old consciousness as an awareness of the environment. What they're interested in is 'consciousness of consciousness': what Mead calls 'self-consciousness.'"

"Keep going," Natasha says. I try to keep a straight face, as I know she would not be pleased if I found her seriousness amusing.

"Let me go back to Mead," I say. "There's a conversation of gestures, such as occurs on a primitive level with feeding the baby. Then there's the internalization of that exchange of gestures."

"Is 'internalization' Mead's word, too, just like Vygotsky's?"

"Yes, certainly, although I think it's worth noting that they differ from their predecessors in that usage. I mean, when Durkheim and Weber talk about 'internalization,' they generally mean just the internalization of *authority*, the internalization of *controls*. When Mead and Vygotsky and Piaget use the word, they mean the conversion of the external behavioral process into an internal thinking process."

"So," says Natasha, "first we have gesture–response behavior, then we have thinking—"

"Wait, not so fast," I protest. "Thinking isn't the result of just *any* gesture–response behavior. If a dog guarding his bone barks defiantly and another dog barks back, they don't then proceed to internalize their barking so that it becomes thinking. But if I order a menacing intruder out of my house, then my words, 'This is my property' have the same meaning for me as they have for him. We share the meaning of what I say: In effect, we together think that meaning."

Natasha grimaces. "Okay, so *now* we have thinking. What next?"

"Next is the emergence of the self, according to Mead. What is peculiar about his conception of the self is that it is strictly cognitive. It is totally involved with our thinking."

"But it's not much different with Vygotsky, is it?" Maxim inquires. "The child entering school begins to generalize and systematize. At first, the word *flower* and the word *rose* stand on the same level, but gradually a *system* of subordinate and superordinate concepts develops."

"Right," I agree. "So for Vygotsky, generalization and systematization lead to consciousness, and this leads the child to awareness of his or her own mental processes—in a word, to self-consciousness. For Mead, it is not simply that such consciousness enables one to become aware of one's self, but that the process is one that *generates* one's self."

"Maybe it's the same for Vygotsky but he just doesn't say it," murmurs Natasha.

"Perhaps," I agree. "But they do agree that *abstraction* is utterly essential to the process of self-development they're describing. For Mead, your offering Sergei a spoonful of infant food and, at the same time, opening your mouth is an example of *concrete thought*. But my asserting 'This is my property' is an example of *abstract thinking* because in it I am appealing to the abstract concept of property that everyone in this society, to some extent, entertains and shares. I am not taking just the intruder's attitude toward my assertion: I'm taking the attitude of what Mead calls the 'generalized other.' It is the way property is seen, not by an particular individual, but by the society as a whole — by people *in general*. Only then is rationality involved."

"All right, I see why you call this *abstract thinking*," says Maxim. "But why does Mead say it's strictly cognitive? Why doesn't it involve emotions? Surely when you defy the intruder, when you threaten him with your words, surely that has emotional implications."

"I agree," I answer, "but Mead argues that *I* do not feel threatened by my words any more than a dog feels threatened by his own growling. It is only the power I invoke when I appeal to the generalized other that I respect and the intruder respects in the same fashion. So the cognitive aspects of my response to my own assertion alone contribute to the formation of my self."

Natasha waves her hand vaguely. "One more question. Doesn't Mead have a more concise or crisp characterization of the self than what you've given us so far?"

"Yes, I was coming to that," I say. "We become selves insofar as we become objects to ourselves."

Maxim and Natasha look at each other and shrug. They exchange some phrases in Russian, then resume staring at me, their heads cocked to one side like a pair of spaniels. Despite their deadpan expressions, I feel convinced they know how comical they look to me. "Don't you see," I say, "assuming a point of view outside ourselves from which to scrutinize ourselves — that's what gives us objectivity. And when that point of view itself involves generality or universality, it enables us to think abstractly and to have rational selves."

"What about rules?" Maxim inquires.

"What *about* rules?" I repeat. "Children's play involves them in concrete thinking. They may assume their playmate's attitude toward themselves, but they are not yet thinking in terms of rules. At best, they may be thinking in terms of *roles*: The child plays the role of parent and addresses her playmate who is playing the role of teacher. She then implicitly responds as teacher to what she has said as parent. But with the game come *rules*, and rules represent the generalized other. Mead puts it this way, that 'the game represents the passage in the life of the child from taking the role of others in play to the organized part that is essential to self-consciousness in the full sense of the term.'"

"So," says Natasha, "the abstract is the general, the universal, the rational, the communal, and that is why the child must be familiar with it along with the specific, the particular, and the concrete. I think this helps explain a little better why Vygotsky insists that the ascent starts with the abstract. But where does it end?"

"It seems to me that whether we read either author, we begin with a series of dichotomies: the abstract versus the concrete, the universal versus the particular, the rational versus the nonrational. And the reso-lution of these dichotomies all point in the same direction — in the direction of the reasonable."

Maxim says slowly, "I think I'm beginning to see a sort of symmetry between Vygotsky and Mead — as you present it. I mean, it's there in their approaches, even when their subject-matter is different."

"Like how?" I ask.

"Well, look, they both see the child as detaching herself from the concrete, particularized situation in which she is immersed in childhood and finding herself not only in a different community composed of teachers and peers, but in an abstract, symbolic cosmos as well, a world of general meanings that attach themselves to everything she makes and says and does."

"Okay."

"Yes, and similarly, look at what happens to the word — Vygotsky's unit of meaning. At first, its situation is relatively concrete: It has its being solely in its correspondence or reference to some particular thing. But Vygotsky argues that schooling detaches the word from its concen-tration on that single point and attaches it instead to a generalization. This confers enormous power on the word and on the person who makes use of that word. So the word finds its place as a meaningful particular in a system of language, just as the individual person finds her place in a community of persons."

"I like that," Natasha comments. "But there's something else I've been wanting to bring up. What got you interested in Mead?"

"I'm not sure, but I think I first learned about Mead through a course in metaphysics given at Columbia by Herbert Schneider. I got interested in Mead's philosophy of perspectives and that led me to Justus Buchler, whose first book on judgment came out in 1951. It also led me to C. Wright Mills, who had done his dissertation on Mead. I found talking to Mills about Mead's social psychology more helpful than talking to anyone else. He later co-authored a book, *Character and Social Structure*, that was heavily influenced by Mead's approach."

"That's a nice way of paying homage to someone one respects," Maxim remarks. "But getting back to the Vygotskian approach, I un-derstand that interest in it is beginning to grow by leaps and bounds. Do you think that has any implications for elementary school philos-ophy?"

I shake my head. "So far, educational psychologists are more concerned to reconcile Vygotsky and Piaget than they are to identify educational programs that might be models of Vygotskian ideas put into practice. In fact, even the Vygotskians — I mean those who are enthusiastically committed to him and not just those who are willing to admit, if grudgingly, that he has a point — are pretty far as yet from having such a perception. Still, one can detect glimmers of light here and there. For example, I've been enjoying this very nice anthology called *Vygotsky and Education*, edited by Luis C. Moll. It came out in 1990 and contains an essay, 'Teaching Mind in Society: Teaching, Schooling and Literate Discourse,' by Ronald Gallimore and Roland Tharp. Well, the authors have a great deal to say about how teachers can intervene helpfully in the zone of proximate development — through modeling, questioning, providing feedback, and so on. But one mode of intervention that particularly interested me in their account was what they called 'cognitive structuring,' by which they mean 'providing a structure for thinking and acting.' They say, 'Various kinds of cognitive structures can be provided. They can be grand: world views, philosophies, ethical systems, scientific theories and religious theologies. Or they can be as modest as giving a name to a thing.' They then proceed to distinguish between cognitive explanation structures and cognitive processing structures — what corresponds, in our approach, to the distinction between learning philosophy and doing it. Philosophy for Children emphasizes the doing, but that doesn't mean that no learning takes place. End of speech."

"So we come back," says Natasha, "to the point you made many weeks ago, that if utterance is the matrix of thinking and if thinking is what we want to flourish, then we must find ways of stimulating critical and inventive discourse. Skillful thinking will naturally emanate from skillful discussions."

Maxim frowns. "Every art and every craft is composed of skills — technical skills. And one acquires those skills by study and practice. It's not true that you learn to dance by dancing and you learn to sing by singing: You've got to study and practice the moves that dancing and singing incorporate."

Natasha's eyes flash. "But when we disagree, as we do now, we say *why* we disagree: We give reasons and criteria, we argue and make judgments. It's just as he says: Skillful interpersonal dialogue gives rise to skillful intrapersonal reflection. You don't need to study the skills separately or practice them separately. It's the same way you learned to speak as a child: not by being assigned exercises in language-building skills or thinking skills, but by listening to and participating in discussions around the kitchen table."

For a moment, Natasha and Maxim glare at each other, then they look at each other with the amusement of ancient co-conspirators.

Maxim turns to me. "Please," he says with an evocative gesture. "Explain how proficiency in thinking is cultivated, in your opinion."

A student at a nearby table is half-hidden by a stack of textbooks, but I manage to catch his attention and borrow his dictionary. "Look," I say, "I open this 1,500-page book at random and the page I'm looking at begins with the word *reassure* and ends with *recapitulate*. In between are words that refer to all sorts of esoteric objects and creatures, like *rebec* and *rebozo* and *rebus*—things kids may never encounter in their whole lives. On the other hand, look at all the verbs that have to do with verbal and mental performances that we engage in everyday: *reassure, rebuff, rebuke, rebut, recalculate, recall, recant, recap,* and *recapitulate.* My point is that we do these things without being conscious of doing them. In a good, lively discussion, we engage in *recalling* and *rebutting* and *recapitulating*; we may even *reassure, rebuff, rebuke,* and *recant.* To read literature or to engage in dialogue is to call into play vast numbers of mental acts. The mind springs to life. I'm not denying that exercises dealing with particular skills can be useful. But I still maintain that the best way of promoting excellent thinking is by promoting excellent discussion that involves a huge range of thinking skills and mental acts."

It is time now to leave the cafeteria with its clatter of dishes and clamor of student voices, to exit the student center through the reluctantly revolving doors, and to pick up an enthusiastic Sergei, who now walks on ahead, hand in hand with Maxim, the two of them deep in conversation.

I sense that Natasha has slowed her pace somewhat and that she has something she wants to say to me. Finally, she announces, "I have two pieces of good news. The first is that I will have an operation. The doctor thinks my chances are excellent and that it will not come back."

"That's wonderful!" I tell her. "That's really wonderful!"

"The second thing is also very—very personal. I have heard from Mikhail."

"From Mikhail!"

"Yes. He is in Beijing. He followed me there."

"How did you hear from him? What did he say?"

"He sent me a telegram. It had only three words: *I am free.*"

"What do you think he expects of you?"

"He asks nothing of me. But I love him, and he is Sasha's father. I must return to Beijing or he must come here."

"You have your operation to think of. And Maxim."

"Yes," she says with a sigh. Then her face brightens, "And I have a book to write."

TENTH VISIT

Two months pass. I hear nothing from Natasha. I call and leave messages, but there is no word from either her or Maxim.

Then she does call and I find myself again in the dingy vestibule of her apartment house, awaiting the buzzer that answers my ring, then ascending the steep, dark stairs at the top of which I find Maxim awaiting me with open arms. We proceed through the long hall, past the bedroom, the kitchen, the bathroom, another bedroom, and, finally, into the living room itself, with its books and plants, its gleaming samovar and decorative porcelain tiles, its graceful icons and splendid glass case full of shining china.

Natasha does not rise to greet me, but extends her hand. At the same time, she introduces me to the tall, gaunt person who has been standing in the darkest corner of the room, half-hidden by a sprawling, huge-leafed plant. It is Mikhail.

I am determined to be direct. "How are you, Natasha?" I ask.

"I will be well," is her only reply, but it is accompanied by such a smile of reassurance (together with another from Maxim) that I feel confident it will be so.

The samovar is pressed into service, the tea and biscuits and pastries are delicious, and I feel sufficiently warmed and cheered to turn my attention from Natasha to the hollow-cheeked, prematurely bald man who sits silently with his legs crossed at the other end of the room. "Natasha tells me you're related to the philosopher Il'enkov," I remark, trying to find a topic that will be sufficiently neutral but of mutual interest.

"Yes," Mikhail answers, after hesitating long enough to make me wonder if he would answer at all. Then he adds, "My uncle. Committed suicide."

"Davydov quotes him with admiration," I say, "especially with regard to aesthetic perception, where it is important that one see the whole as well as the parts, for this is related to seeing the object from one's own perspective as well as from the perspectives of all the others in one's community. This is what Davydov calls 'imagination.' The practical importance of this, as far as aesthetic education is concerned, is that every skill should be taught for its generic as well as for its subject-specific aspect."

While I am speaking, I am aware that I have gone on too long and have initiated a discussion that is somehow quite inappropriate. Mikhail merely shrugs. I then realize that I had made no comment about the fact that his uncle had committed suicide, although I hadn't known of it previously. All I did was launch into my own, preestablished agenda. My visit, I am beginning to realize, is threatening to turn into a disaster.

Natasha tries to bridge the gap. "I have told Mikhail about Philosophy for Children."

"I wonder if your uncle would have liked it," I hazard.

Mikhail looks up sharply. "He would have hated it. But then, he and I never saw eye to eye about anything. He was a Hegelian and an idealist. I was, in those days, a Carnapian positivist. He hated logic, especially."

"But he was the philosophical link between Davydov and Vygotsky," I protest.

"Yes," says Mikhail, "and in his younger days he was quite lively. He and Zinoviev and Davydov and Nina Yulina, who is now an eminent professor at the Institute of Philosophy, used to spend long evenings together carousing philosophically, making caricatures, reciting poems, and telling jokes. Then things changed."

"Still," I persist, "he continued to see ideals as the fundamental criteria of action. He was critical of Soviet philosophy for not agreeing with him on this point, isn't that so?"

"Yes, this caused him much despondency," Mikhail acknowledges. "But personal feelings also entered in. There was his wife, Olga, to be considered and his daughter, Helena. She is my cousin, as you know, and today she has a family of her own."

"Was your situation connected in any way with your uncle's?"

"No, not at all. The KGB suspected me of being a dissident and they knew, through informers, of my relationship with Natasha. Then my wife died under mysterious circumstances. I had nothing to do with it, but they called me in and explained to me the case they could create against me. I felt trapped because there was no way in which I could prove my innocence. I could see that they would have no hesitation in putting me away for the rest of my life in a prison camp in Siberia."

"But they offered you a deal?"

"Yes, they promised not to make a case against me if Natasha and I would perform a few nasty little chores for them. We agreed. Then they broke their part of the bargain and put me away for five years anyhow." His long, morose face breaks into a grin. "It took me a while to trace Natasha and Sasha, but I have them now and nothing will ever separate us again."

Natasha nods. "Nothing," she echoes. "Mikhail is already working on a book," she adds. "It's tentatively entitled, *Bakhtin on Text*."

"Ah!" I exclaim. "A Bakhtinite!"

"Just another Mikhail, I'm afraid," Mikhail answers diffidently. "Bakhtin is the first person to have seen the profound implications of the text — the metaphysics and epistemology of the text, if you will."

I respond, "But how? I mean, how does he do it?"

"Well," says Mikhail, getting another cup of tea from the samovar and pausing maddeningly as he stirs his sugar, "he begins by defining a text as 'any coherent complex of signs.' And so, just as we have thoughts about our thoughts, we have texts about texts. Indeed, if we are to do any serious thinking about thinking, 'the text is the only possible point of departure.'"

Natasha intervenes. "What Bakhtin sees is that every text is an utterance and every utterance is defined by its plan and by its way of realizing that plan."

I frown. "I'm afraid I don't follow you —" I begin.

Now it is Maxim's turn to intervene. "Look," he explains, "this is the first principle of textology. Every text involves the creation of a second, framing text, and that framing text itself has a second author."

Mikhail tries to say something, but Natasha intercedes again: "Don't you see, the text is a kind of monad that reflects all texts. Every text has a dialogical relationship with every other text and behind every text stands a language."

The three of them stare at me intently. "I'm becoming very confused," I confess.

"Please," says Mikhail to Natasha and Maxim, "let me. Every text has two aspects. One aspect is the text insofar as it is repeatable or translatable. The other is the text insofar as it is irreproducible or unique. Everything repeatable is linked to the language system from which it comes. Everything unique is linked to the author."

"Well —" Natasha says doubtfully, "everything repeatable is linked to its plan and to the realization of that plan, as means are linked to ends."

Now Maxim is shaking his head vigorously. "Don't you see," he says to Natasha, "even when the text is reproduced, that very reproduction becomes a new, unrepeatable event in the life of the text?"

Mikhail spreads his hands over the coffee table. "For Bakhtin," he says carefully, "the text can never be completely translated. There is no potential single text of texts."

Maxim downs the remainder of his cup of tea in a single gulp and says excitedly, "I want to come back to what I was saying about the framing text. The framing text is the context of the text—the context that involves the questioning, the refuting, the entire inquiry into the text. And so this dialogue develops between the two texts that meet, and this dialogue is the transcription of the thinking that goes on in all of the human sciences."

Finally, Natasha raises her arm. "Enough!" she cries out. "Enough! Mikhail, I hear Sasha beginning to wake up. Go bring him in!"

Sergei enters, rubbing his eyes. He pauses doubtfully at the door, stares at me for a moment, then rushes to his mother and buries his face in her shoulder. But I can see that he still manages to peek out at me through the corner of one eye.

I reach over to Sergei and manage to shake his hand, which seems very tiny in contrast with Mikhail's. "I must go," I announce.

The three adults shake their heads. "Impossible!" Natasha exclaims. "I've been telling Mikhail all about Philosophy for Children, and he has all sorts of questions to ask you about it. Please don't stand up. Sit down. Have another cup of tea. Have some more cookies—they're delicious, if I say so myself!"

I sit down, mumbling something or other.

Natasha continues, "I would like Mikhail's introduction to Philosophy for Children to be something different. Not just the reading of a text in which it's his text about your text or my thinking about your thinking—"

I begin to suspect the direction of Natasha's thinking, so I interrupt with: "What do you have in mind?"

She says, looking at me very directly, "You choose a selection and let us script-read it."

"Very well," I agree. "Do you have a copy of *Suki*?"

She reaches over to a shelf behind the sofa and plucks a worn copy of *Suki* from a complete set of the curriculum. As I turn to page 57, I say, "Natasha, you be Suki. Mikhail, you be Mr. Tong and Ann. Maxim, you be the grandfather and the grandmother. Sergei, you be Kyo. And I'll be narrator." This is the text we then proceed to act out:

Suki had two living grandparents, but she had never met them. Her father rarely ever mentioned them, although they lived on a farm not far away — no more then 3 or 4 hours by car. Suki was quite surprised when her father, after opening the mail, waved an envelope rather vaguely in her direction and announced, "They want us to come see them."

"Who."

"Your grandparents."

"Oh." Suki thought for a moment, then asked, "Are they okay?"

"They don't exactly say, but my guess is that maybe they're not."

Again, Suki said, "Oh." Her face clouded over a bit. "When would we go?"

"We could make the whole trip, there and back, in a day, so I guess we can go this coming Saturday."

"Dad, it'll be good to meet them and to see the farm, but — " she paused for a moment. "Do you think it would be all right if I asked a friend to come along?"

"I certainly have no objection and I don't think they would mind. Which friend would you ask?"

"To a farm? I don't know — Millie would enjoy it, I'm sure. But I think I'll ask Anne first."

Anne clapped her hands when Suki spoke to her. "Grrreat! I'm sick of hanging around the house weekends!"

Suki nodded. She had some misgivings about the trip, but she didn't share them with Anne. She especially wondered what her grandparents would be like.

When they left Saturday morning at dawn, it was crisp and chilly. The hours in the car passed quickly. Anne and Suki, sitting together in the back seat, sang songs for a while, played "Ghost," and then, using some sheets of paper from Anne's sketch pad, played "Battleship." Kio curled up on the front seat, his head on his father's lap, and slept.

They left the main highway and traveled some miles through a forest. Then the road branched and they took a dirt road that ran up to the crest of a hill. Suddenly, they could see for miles; the land fell away, stretching out in patches of farmland that reminded Anne of a collage she had made of bits of burlap, corduroy and hopsacking. Just beyond the crest, surrounded by a white rail fence on three sides and a stone fence on the fourth, some small outbuildings and a chickenhouse. But there was also the charred remains of a great barn that had burnt to the ground.

Suki had expected her grandparents to be elderly, tired-looking, and uncomfortable with young people — and she was right. But she quickly became accustomed to her grandfather's gruffness and her grandmother's reticence. "That's just her way," she explained to Anne.

Suki's grandfather took them on a tour of the farm. He led the way, followed by Kio, holding his father's hand, with Suki and Anne, their arms about each other's waists for a brief moment, farther back. In addition to the chickens, there were two cows and a horse. The girls giggled when they saw the horse because it had a tiny mustache which gave it a very dapper and distinguished look. But it was Suki's grandfather that Anne found most interesting.

"I'd love to sketch him," she told Suki as they were walking towards the henhouse. "His forehead slopes straight back from his nose like George Washington's. But he has that square sort of beard that Abraham Lincoln had."

Suki smiled, then remarked, "Patriotic geometry! You'll need a ruler to draw him!"

The first room inside the henhouse contained sacks of grain. Suki's grandfather spoke to her directly for the first time: "Like to give the chickens some scratch?"

"What's scratch?"

"Oh, mainly cracked corn and oats with some barley thrown in. I usually give it to them late in the afternoon, but they'd like some now, I'm sure." He filled a pail with the mixture and Kio and the girls took turns throwing handfuls to the chickens. "Better check the water pails while we're here," he added, half to himself. There was a handpump in the corner of the grain room. Primed with half a bucket of water and pumped vigorously, it soon made loud, gasping sounds and, before long, spouted water into the pail.

Kio and the girls were fascinated. They had never seen a handpump before, having taken it for granted that water always came from faucets.

"Let me! Let me!" Kio exclaimed, and his grandfather let him pump the handle. He soon learned the rhythm of lifting the handle and pushing it down again so as to bring forth a full gush of water. They went back outside and Suki's grandfather showed them where he split kindling wood, where the apple cellar was located, and where he kept a compost pile at the corner of the meadow. They visited the egg cellar and the machine shed. Kio was fascinated by the tractor and the harvesting equipment.

Finally, they wound their way back up the path to the house. In the living room, the great stone fireplace had been lit and Suki, Anne and Kio stood warming themselves in front of it, slowly rotating as if on individual spits. They were hungry and the food, when it came, was so delicious they almost couldn't recognize it. The bread, the milk, the eggs, the butter, the vegetables — every taste was fresh, distinct and intense.

"It's as if the food we usually eat is just a pale copy of this food," Suki remarked. "Compared to the milk we get at home, this is real milk! And these eggs taste like eggs ought to taste — like real eggs!"

Her grandfather permitted himself a slight smile, although it threatened for a moment to fracture his face. Then he lit his pipe and relaxed. "Well, son, what do you think?" he asked, addressing Kio. "Would you like to be a farmer some day?"

Kio's mouth was full of blueberry muffin and his "I don't know" came out sounding like "ow-no."

"Are you going to rebuild the barn?" Mr. Tong asked.

Suki saw her grandfather redden, but he merely remarked, "I don't think so."

Her grandmother leaned over to Mr. Tong and said, "It just about killed him — that fire."

Suki watched the flames in the fireplace. In her imagination she saw the great barn ablaze and her grandmother restraining her grandfather. "Fire," she said to herself. Other images thronged into her mind, the pump, the bracing autumn air, the soft turf of the meadow. "Earth, air, fire and water," she thought.

"It went up like tinder," said Suki's grandfather. "That's wood for you. Can't trust it. You can only trust stone. I'll use stone, if I ever build another one."

"Ah," mused Mr. Tong, "wood never betrays us, although sometimes perhaps we betray it. When I'm planning a piece of oak or walnut, or while I'm sanding them or rubbing them down with steel wool, I remember that they were once parts of living trees. Any piece of wood you pick up, like this table top here, or these chairs — it's wood that was once alive. Even now it has a warmth to it that stone never has. Wood is live, but stone is — stone is — " he paused, unsure about completing his thought.

"Even wood petrifies," the farmer responded. "Sooner or later, everything turns to stone."

"Suki," said Kio, "you know that sea shell you have at home? It's stone and it was once alive."

"Well, it's not exactly stone, Kio. But daddy, how about that coral necklace you once gave me? How about coral reefs? Weren't they once alive?"

Before Mr. Tong could answer, his mother-in-law commented, "Of course everything changes. That's nature. But what's this about everything turning to stone? Nonsense! Everything changes — vegetation turns into mulch and mulch turns back into plants again. Only change is constant."

Her husband responded: "I saw and planed every board in that barn. Now it's all ashes and those ashes are not going to turn back into a barn. Use stone, I say. Build things to last forever."

The room fell quiet. Anne had felt somewhat like an eavesdropper during the entire conversation. She found the silence almost unbearable. She became aware that a clock was ticking in a nearby room. Silently, she counted the beats, hoping that a chime would mark the quarter-hour.

Suki's grandmother spoke up again, a flash of fire in her eyes,

"What will be, will be. But don't confuse our job and nature's. Nature's job is change—forever turning one thing into another, never knowing or asking why. But our job's turning the world into poetry!"

Startled, Suki looked up and found her grandmother looking at her.

"Your father tells me you write poetry, Suki."

Suki tried to say something, but she only murmured something unintelligible.

"I did too, when I was your age, and for a good many years afterwards." Suki's grandmother glanced at her husband and sighed. "It's funny, though. I have a photo album full of snapshots, but I can't stand to look at them. When I see them, I shake my head and say, 'That's not me!' But I still go over the poetry—I read it and reread it. It's just as fresh as when I first wrote it. And I say to myself, 'If I'm anywhere, it's here in these words.'"

"Maybe you didn't know it, but your mother wrote poetry too," Suki's grandfather added.

Suddenly Suki had a very clear image of her mother.

"I didn't much approve of it, but she went on writing anyhow," he added.

Suki's grandfather and grandmother exchanged glances. Suki's grandmother got up, went to the chest of drawers in the corner, and got out a sheaf of papers in a folder. "We want you to have them," she said, handing the poems to Suki. Suki's grandfather nodded his approval.

Suki hugged the poems. She rose, silently kissed and hugged each of her grandparents, then returned to hugging the poems. She knew she didn't want to read them until she was safely alone, at home.

Later, as they were leaving, she tried to tell her grandparents how much their gift meant to her. They nodded and replied, "Just don't be so long about coming back."

Mr. Tong shook his mother-in-law's hand warmly. "I'm going to think about what you said, that our job's turning the world into poetry."

"Oh," she replied with a smile, looking at Suki and Kio. "You seem to be off to a pretty good start already."

As Maxim finishes the last line of the selection, Sergei utters a squeal of appreciation and jumps in his lap. But all the while he keeps looking at Mikhail.

"Well," says Mikhail, to no one in particular, "from the monological to the dialogical and from the literary to the philosophical."

"Ah," I add, "from the text to the context and from the context to the community of inquiry."

"No!" Natasha protests, "the context here *is* the community of inquiry!"

I throw up my hands as if to say, "I shall not be an obstacle. Let the conversation proceed unchecked!" I cannot tell them how touched I am by their recitation of the episode from *Suki*. And once again, the aria from *La Traviata* runs through my mind.

Natasha's eyes are large and luminous in her ashen face as she turns to me and remarks, "It now seems so long ago that we talked about higher-order thinking." I nod and she continues, "You said at the time that higher-order thinking was the result of the interpenetration of critical and creative thinking." Again, I nod, but this time I say, "You find that unsatisfactory?"

"It leaves values out of account," she observes. "Like compassion. Like gratitude. Like love."

It is Mikhail's turn to speak up, and he does so with an air of wondering: "In those years in which Natasha and I were separated, I thought about her constantly and I just as continually cared about her." A faint smile curls Natasha's lips and she murmurs, "Same here."

"But as time went on," Mikhail says, "the thinking and the caring drew closer together, until they were indistinguishable. Was I mistaken to have thought that way?" His voice is gentle and wondering in tone.

Maxim asks, "Do you mean, 'Could some thinking be a caring and some caring a thinking?' Aren't the thoughts of the grandparents caring thoughts and aren't their carings thoughtful carings?"

Mikhail shrugs and embraces Natasha more tightly. "I was trying to say that critical and creative thinking alone are not enough. A values dimension must be added. We must drill our way down until we find the wellspring of all values and incorporate that wellspring in our thinking."

Natasha kisses him and comments gravely, "Thinking and emotions are not necessarily opposed to one another. Caring, for example, is both a form of thinking and a form of emotion. If we can think critically and creatively, we can also think caringly."

"Those are the three chief aspects of higher-order thinking?" I ask. Then I add, "How stupid of me! Of course that's so! In our development of philosophical curriculum materials for children, those three dimensions have always been presupposed, even if they were not articulated theoretically." It is now far later than I had planned to stay, so I prepare to leave. I shake hands with Maxim, then with Mikhail and then with Natasha. We also touch cheeks.

"Come, Sergei, give me a big hug!" I demand. But Sergei seems abashed and rushes to his mother.

Natasha calls out to me, "Keep up your work!" Then she adds, somewhat more softly, "Be good!" As I turn to leave she says, still more softly, and with a mischievous chuckle, "Farewell, my reciprocal inquirer!"

AFTERWORD

A Comparison Between the Philosophy for Children Approach and the Cultural-Historical and Activity Approaches: Psychological and Educational Foundations

ARKADY A. MARGOLIS

Director, Department of Teacher Education,
Institute of Psychology, Russian Academy of Education,
and Rector, International College of Education, Moscow

One of the most interesting approaches in twentieth century psychology, little known to Western scholars, is the activity approach. It is an outcome of the cultural-historical theory conceived by Lev Vygotsky between 1924 and 1930 in Russia but left incomplete because of his death. The ideas connected with this theory greatly influenced a number of prominent Russian and foreign scholars and were further developed into the activity theory by one of Vygotsky's most talented followers, A. N. Leont'ev.

Recognizing the importance of this approach, proponents of the activity theory developed theoretical views on specific forms of human activity. A significant study of one of the most important activities — the learning activity — was prepared by D. B. El'konin and Vasily Davydov, who have been working on the activity theory since the 1960s.

We believe this theory has a strong creative potential and interesting applications in the area of developmental instruction and therefore merits a more detailed description of its most important features. In attempting to understand new models of education based on dialogue, such as "developmental education," it would be productive to compare it to the Western Philosophy for Children model with which it shares many similar goals.

VYGOTSKY'S CULTURAL AND HISTORICAL THEORIES

As is well known, Vygotsky concentrated on investigating the origins and development of cultural forms of human behavior and on discovering specifically human psychological functions. Several key concepts conceived by him and his colleagues provide a framework for his theory:

1. The first concept, which is related to the so-called mediated character of human psychological functions, regards sociohistorical experience and the collective activity of individuals as instrumental in building new and higher levels of psychological functioning.

2. The process by which cultural signs are adopted is significant in the person's transition to a higher level of psychological functioning. Vygotsky defined these sign functions and the ways they were transmitted very broadly. He interpreted these signs as specific "psychological tools" that help people organize their behavior and actions and teach them to guide their behavior and actions at will.

3. Education is determined through a process of sign adoption. Signs that are initially independent from social origins (but always have social origins) are transformed from an external to an internal form (in the context of the *process of internalization*), thereby guaranteeing a self-regulative (or autoregulative) quality to a person's actions and behavior.

4. The specific tool-like role of signs is related (according to the cultural-historical theory) to the fact that while emerging seminally in a process of "child–adult" interaction (as a medium of this interaction and as a tool guided by the partner's behavior), they are transformed during internalization within the thinking activity medium and as a tool guided by the person's own behavior.

5. In Vygotsky's work, this mechanism was defined as a genetic law of cultural development. According to this law, every mental function appears on the scene twice and in two ways: first, socially, interpersonally, or interpsychologically, and second, psychologically, inside the child's mind, that is, intrapsychologically.

6. Attempting to understand what role education plays in the context of development led Vygotsky to conclude that a solid education can play a role and help push forward the locomotive of child development. In other words, education must not be merely adequate to the actual level of the child's development; on the contrary, education should precede the actual level of development, through constructing the so-called zone of proximal development on the basis of specific interactions

between children and adults and children with one another. The ideas listed above laid the foundations for Vygotsky's cultural-historical theory of psychological functional development.

LEONT'EV'S ACTIVITY THEORY

During the period when this theory was being proposed, a number of concurrent research studies demonstrated the important role that object-related activity plays in understanding the development of behavior and thinking. These studies were continued by one of Vygotsky's closest followers and proponents, A. N. Leont'ev. The results of Leont'ev's research showed that mental reflection in humans is deeply and internally connected to and mediated by the process of human activity. Thus the self-regulative quality in a person's behavior is mainly constructed and realized in the depth of the activity process. According to Leont'ev, the object of this activity appears twice in the process: first, independently from the person (the subject of the activity), as an object that guides and transforms human activity directly without any mediation, and second, as an image (or a concept) of this object, as a product of its mental reflection, which appears as a result of a person's activity.

At the same time, the concept of internalization and the general genetic law of cultural development of psychological functions, as portrayed by the activity theory, are formed. The content of the genetic law was interpreted as a transition from an initial, object-related and socially shared form of "child–adult" joint activity to an intrapsychological, internal form (connected through the basic principle of their structural similarity).

In this study, Leont'ev accurately analyzed an integrative human activity structure, selected and examined activity components (such as necessity and motive, object of the activity, actions and their goal, operation, etc.), and studied the relationship among these components. A number of subsequent studies showed that the activity components are constantly and mutually transformed from one to the other.

THE LEARNING ACTIVITY THEORY OF EL'KONIN AND DAVYDOV

The subsequent development of the cultural-historical activity approach, from about 1960, was mainly linked (as stated above) to El'konin and Davydov's design of the learning activity theory. The main premise of this theory is that the goal of the learning activity (including joint "adult–children" activity) is the learning itself. In other words, the primary goal of instruction is to teach students the skills necessary "to learn on their own."

The learning task of these goals is strongly dependent on the structure of the learning activity and on the full realization of all its necessary components in educational practice. The principal elements of this structure are an instructional task (or learning task), instructional (learning) actions, and such actions as control and evaluation.

According to Davydov, a learning task is learning how to find general solutions to particular and basic problems. A student who is solving a problem as a learning task is first directed to search for the most general structural principle of a studied object (or searching for its unique mode of development), while a student who is solving the problem concretely or pragmatically is mainly directed to the actual solving of the task.

According to the learning activity theory, problem-solving is dependent on a process of learning actions, which include:

- Transformation of the learning situation (or the object of learning) in order to reveal and discover the object's general structural principle, or its key relation
- Modeling of the discovered principle in a graphic or sign-symbolic form
- Transformation of the object model for the purpose of studying its principal properties and features separately from other additional object relations
- Deduction and building of a series of specific concrete and pragmatic tasks that can be solved with the help of a generalized approach of the student's activity
- Control over the performance of preceding actions
- Evaluation of the adoption of the generalized approach

The carrying out of these transformations could guarantee, on the one hand, that task-solving becomes the only solution for a learning task and, on the other hand, that the student's action acquires a form of learning actions along with the grasp of the object of study. As a result, a student will learn how to think theoretically about the object of study and, by doing this, he or she will form an appropriate theoretical concept about this object.

The developmental model of education, which is based on this theory, is primarily aimed at constructing theoretical thinking about the content of various school subjects, such as mathematics, language, arts, etc.

In Russia of today, this system of education is one of the most productive alternatives to the so-called traditional school system, which is mainly aimed at a direct delivery of ready knowledge and training with certain specific skills.

A child's educational development based on learning activity is mediated through the content of specific subjects. This has some advantages but also some drawbacks. One of the most notable drawbacks results from the difficulty of distinguishing between the student's own learning actions (such as transformation of the object of study, modeling, transformation of a model, etc.) related to his or her analytical and synthetic activity and actions developed on the basis of the content of the material. These and some other difficulties have greatly restricted numerous attempts to develop children's thinking not through the content of specific school subjects but directly and without any relation to particular disciplines.

The presence of these problems in Russian education have inhibited many attempts to create courses in philosophy and logic and to implement them in Russian schools. The proponents of these attempts usually assume that the study of philosophy as a school subject is in itself developmentally influential without the use of any methodology. The first examples of such courses, dating back to the years after World War II, were short-lived and were eventually recast into courses such as "Knowledge of Society," which taught philosophy as a series of Marxist ideological declarations and were widespread in Russian education from the 1970s up to the 1990s.

Simultaneously with the many economic and political changes in Russian society, there developed a strong interest in teaching philosophy as an elementary school subject. However, most philosophy courses in Russian schools today are either copies of university-level courses or introductions to the history of philosophy. Both approaches use traditional education methods that are inadequate for developing children's thinking skills.

One of the best programs truly aimed at the development of thinking being implemented in Russia in the mid-1990s is based on the Philosophy for Children program from the Institute for the Advancement of the Philosophy for Children from Montclair State University, directed by Professor Matthew Lipman and his colleagues.

PHILOSOPHY FOR CHILDREN

The features of this program pertinent to our comparative analysis are the following:

1. One of the main educational goals of the philosophy curriculum in school settings is the development of a student's ability to make logically correct judgments so as to facilitate reflective and critical behavior and reasoning.
2. The creators of this program consider philosophy to be an effective tool and method for improving and developing a person's thinking.
3. Teaching philosophy should be a special educational methodology different from traditional disciplines.

Other important aspects of the program reflect the interface of philosophical inquiry, cognitive development, and the learning process:

1. The starting point for Lipman's theory concludes with the supposition that the logical development of a child must become a special task; the spontaneous development of logical operations in simply growing up is not enough for successful learning in school.
2. It is too late to strengthen logical thinking in high school or college. The most sensitive age span for philosophical reasoning is 6–10, when the child's intellectual curiosity is very strong.
3. It is not possible to study philosophy (or to do philosophy) in a standard academic way. On the contrary, philosophy is a result of personal intellectual attempts — a result of the student's thinking about the world and about thinking itself. Such thinking is supposed to be organized and facilitated by the teacher.
4. The goal of the learning process is not to develop several separate thinking skills but to develop thinking as an integrated process, as a whole entity. The main features of thinking as a process are:

- Self-correction
- Sensitivity to a context
- Ability to make judgments
- Basing judgments on criteria rather than rules

5. In attempting to develop children's thinking, the Philosophy for Children course must have at least two major components: a child's thinking about the surrounding world (cognitive component) and simultaneous thinking about thinking itself (metacognitive compo-

nent) — that is, assuming different ways and perspectives of thinking, points of view, hidden assumptions, and so on.

6. Discussing philosophical problems instead of reading about them and their solutions is doing real philosophy.

7. Socratic dialogues are not only an antitheses to the traditional lectures-and-answers format but also a mechanism of group and individual development, a tool for achieving the declared developmental goal for children's thinking and reasoning.

8. The development of individual thinking is a product of internalization of group thinking as demonstrated in collective discourse. One psychological mechanism for doing this (described by Vygotsky) is the following: Correcting a partner's way of reasoning and method of reasoning through a dialogue or collective discussion develops a way of reasoning for the whole group of students, which, when internalized improves the individual reasoning of each individual student.

9. The creation of a communication-oriented learning environment during Philosophy for Children classes leads to two important results. Logic skills acquired through discussion are applied as criteria for selecting correct conclusions and judgments and are instruments of reasoning that can guarantee development of thinking skills. Parallel to this development of thinking, an important change takes place in the students: They shift from just talking to discussing philosophically. In other words, they develop into a community of inquiry, characterized by

- An interest in discussing philosophical problems
- Collective discussion on the basis of logical rules and procedures
- Internalization of collectively constructed ways and models of reasoning
- Self-corrective character of the collective style of group thinking
- Ability to make judgments

10. Because the philosophical content must be made interesting and understandable to children, it is presented in the form of a novel, the main characters of which are trying to solve age-appropriate and, at the same time, philosophically real problems. The text is the most essential part of the curriculum, consisting of a series of novels covering different issues related to certain areas of philosophy (metaphysics, logic, ethics, aesthetics, and so on) in an attractive (age-appropriate) form.

In the Philosophy for Children program, text not only serves as the source for philosophical questions and ensuing discussions in a classroom, but also has the capability of building different models for discussion, reasoning, and thinking. The last point also means that students in this program (in comparison to those with traditional curricula) have more models of thinking than usual (not only does the teacher serve as a model, but the text provides thinking and reasoning models that are taken from an existing culture). The text is also a model community of inquiry since its community consists of characters that function in the children's novel.

11. The teacher plays a very unusual role in the Philosophy for Children program. The teacher is neither an expert in the content of study (as in other school subjects) nor a judge who evaluates the students' thoughts and statements. The teacher in this program is, first of all, an organizer of philosophical dialogues and discussions, a facilitator of collective reasoning and the group's (as well as the individuals') thinking. In principle, the teacher cannot be the judge, since, in contrast to a subject such as mathematics, there are no correct answers to philosophical problems. The major task of a teacher in this program is to organize the type of discussion that allows participants to acquire some discussion rules and some approaches to possible solutions of the problem being discussed.

12. The points mentioned above are also important when they are applied to the training of teachers for the Philosophy for Children curriculum. To prepare a teacher with a style and mode of teaching that advances the program's educational goals, a specific model of teacher training (very different from the traditional one) must be designed.

COMPARING THE PHILOSOPHY OF CHILDREN CURRICULUM TO THE DEVELOPMENTAL MODEL OF EDUCATION (BASED ON THE CULTURAL-HISTORICAL APPROACH)

A comparative analysis of the major educational goals and specific features of both programs indicates a significant number of similarities between them:

1. *Education as a tool of development of a child's thinking.* Both programs agree with the Vygotskian concept of education, which sees education as the locomotive of the child's development, rather than the Piagetian position, which maintains that it is necessary to teach only those concepts that are appropriate to a child's actual level of development.

2. *Social origins of the developmental process.* Both approaches strongly support the need to create the kind of social conditions that will be

productive in the learning process. In other words, individual development in a social situation of learning is a result of group development.

3. *Role of internalization.* In both theoretical frameworks, the process
of internalization plays a specific role in transforming group development (coming from social situations of learning or, specifically, a constructed collective learning activity of students and teacher, children
and adult) into the individual development of a child.

4. *Education is activity.* This point, to some extent common to both
programs, means that education in constructed as a specific form of
student activity (the so-called learning activity in Davydov's approach
and community of inquiry discussion dialogues in Lipman's). This, in
turn, determines the specific content, form, and even method of education. In Davydov's approach, not every kind of education can be called
a learning activity — only those kinds that involve solving learning tasks
(finding the most general way of solving the same tasks by a whole
class) through the use of the learning activity (transformation of the
object, modeling, changing of a model, and so on). Similarly, Philosophy for Children assumes that only philosophical discourse and dialogue, specifically organized by a teacher — not *any* kind of student
talking — will fulfill the program's educational objectives. Doing philosophy instead of reading about it is essential to the activity approach.

5. *Development of thinking.* The development of children's thinking
that stems from the learning activity in Davydov's approach is analo-
gous to the development of children's reasoning and ability to form
good judgments stemming from the philosophical discussions in the
Philosophy for Children program. In both cases, the originators assume
that a common environment does not stimulate development of theoretical and formal reasoning without a purposefully constructed methodology.

6. *Nonauthoritarian position of the teacher.* The development of children's thinking (either theoretical or formal reasoning) needs a learning
environment in which children either necessarily discover theoretical
concepts in objects of study (Davydov) or collectively formulate and
construct definitions of a philosophical problem that is discussed in the
classroom. In both cases, this would be impossible with a teacher who
supplied students with ready solutions and answers. It also means that
in both programs the teacher is more of a facilitator and organizer of
the learning activity and discussion than would be the case in a traditional setting.

7. *Hypothesis concerning the starting point.* A careful examination of
both approaches indicates a similar basic hypothesis. El'konin and Davydov's nontraditional formulation states that education that uses learn-

ing activity to form theoretical thinking should not be implemented in
secondary schools — rather, theoretical concepts within a framework of
developmental education should be introduced to elementary school
children, since at that age they are more sensitive to theoretical concepts stemming from the learning activity (according to El'konin's peri-
odic age divisions). Lipman's approach is very close to this hypothesis.
Philosophical problems that have traditionally not been taught until
high school — and most often taught only in universities — have moved
down significantly, first to middle schools, then to elementary schools,
and now to kindergartens. Children are motivated to participate in
and are interested by discussions of philosophical problems. They are
amazed by them, sensitive to them, and capable of discussing them at
a preschool and elementary school age.

In addition to these similarities and commonalities, we can also
point out several differences between the Philosophy for Children and
developmental education programs:

1. When speaking about thinking (as a whole process rather than
separate cognitive actions and operations) as a primary educational
goal, Lipman speaks about the necessity to develop a formal way of
thinking and reasoning based on logical rules stemming from the Aristotelian tradition, whereas Davydov does not pay any attention to formal reasoning. Davydov does not consider formal reasoning essential
to the formation of theoretical thinking (since it is actually quite the
opposite of theoretical thinking, according to the dialectical tradition).
Moreover, Davydov considers the development of formal reasoning to
stem from the empirical experience of a preschooler, which is completed
at the moment of entering an elementary school. In other words, according to Davydov, theoretical thinking must be formed through specific education based on the learning activity of students, whereas activity theorists maintain that formal reasoning is a result of children's
actual growth and does not require any special intervention by the
teacher or any specific curriculum.

Recognizing that some arguments of the activity theory proponents
are true, we must also admit that real educational practice often shows
us that elementary school children are not prepared to participate in a
learning activity that is deeply connected to the formation and use of
mental actions such as analysis, synthesis, reflection, and so on, just
because their basic level of formal thinking (finding similarities, drawing distinctions, constructing hypotheses and analogies) is still un-

formed. This also means that the sharpening of such skills must be the subject of specific work by both the students and the teacher.

2. Davydov's model of the educational process and learning activities differs from Lipman's. When Davydov speaks about learning activities he means that the initial form of the subject(student)-object interaction is a hands-on activity. That kind of object transformation carried on by students permits them to discover the most essential developmental relationship that is uniform for a whole class of objects, like a "cell" from which a group of organisms might be deduced and reconstructed. Lipman assumes discourse—verbal interactions among students, facilitated by a teacher—to be the most important (but not the only) form of collective learning activity in a Philosophy for Children classroom.

3. The object of study is different in the two programs. This is an extremely significant distinction from our point of view because of the major effects that follow.

The developmental model of education mainly deals with scientific objects (stemming from different scientific disciplines). The common feature among them is the presence of the object's internal principle, a major and most important rule that is neutral to a subject (including the student) and that is discovered and reconstructed in a theoretical concept form through a process of student and teacher learning activity and as a result of a subject–object interaction.

The scientific or theoretical method of interaction implies use of different scientific tools, such as systems, schema, maps, models, and so on (signs in a broad meaning), which mediate this interaction and transform it into (according to Vygotsky) a cultural form. Signs that mediate subject–object interaction in a classroom (in math, language, or anything else) are not invented by the students—they already exist in culture and science. They are internalized through a group activity of reconstructing the object of study, restructuring the object of study, restructuring the very way of children's thinking and, thereby, ensuring their development.

The same process is very different in the Philosophy for Children program. The object of study, in this case, is not a specific, concrete scientific fact of a scientific discipline. On the contrary, it is the most general relationship and universal scheme covering the whole picture of the world and of human beings in the world. For more than 2,000 years, different philosophical schools have argued about the most essential philosophical problems, and this dialogue is not and cannot be completed.

Therefore in this case we have an object that strongly differs from the one that functions in developmental education. There is no certain principle or rule that might be discovered as a final answer to a certain philosophical problem. There are no final and absolute answers. Answers are true in a certain context, in a certain way of thinking, based on an appropriate axiom, which might become false if the context were changed.

In other words, each philosophical definition might be correct only within a certain context, which, in turn, means that each rule discovered by students (as a result of a discussion organized by a teacher) is a kind of convention of the discussion participants.

Specific ways of establishing the children's conventions fixed in a certain definition that is true in one context and might be false in another involve not only the process of internalization (which can stimulate individual development on the basis of group achievements) but also (and probably more importantly) the process of externalization that helps build new and more advanced group definitions on the basis of individual personal externalized ideas and representations of philosophical problems.

This mechanism is strongly linked to a two-way road of an externalization–internalization process, much more so than we see in the developmental model of education, for example. There is no place for children's preconceptions in developmental education. They are false, developmentalists say, and must yield to scientific (theoretical) concepts about the object of study. Specifically constructed, hands-on, joint activity involving students and teacher destroys "wrong" preconceptions (at least from the point of view of the originators of this approach) and, through the mediation of different sign-symbolic tools, permits the reconstruction of an object of study in the "proper" only correct way. "Resistance" of an object stimulates the children's way of thinking, which concludes in the construction of a theoretical concept and the child's development.

In Philosophy for Children one cannot find any natural object with only one possible functioning and reconstructive principle. Instead, there is a philosophical problem that can be thought about in numerous ways. All students' preconceptions about this problem are externalized, verbally objectified and articulated in a group discussion, and transformed in the process of group reflection. Here the mechanism of development is not the student–object interaction, not even the one mediated by sign-symbolic tools that is later internalized, but rather student-student interaction and students' exchange of ideas and representations of a philosophical problem. Criticizing a partner's way of thinking by using certain procedures (questioning, logical rules, arguments, finding out hidden assumptions) teaches one to subsequently apply the same tools of inquiry to one's own way and model of thinking. The more advanced, collectively constructed way of group reasoning that is internalized stimulates individual development of student thinking. Reflection results not from the inadequacy of a child's preconception of an object of study, but rather from a dialogue with other preconceptions about the same philosophical problem.

NOTE

Translated from the Russian by Arkady A. Margolis and Marina Cunningham.

BIBLIOGRAPHY

These references are very selective. Not all the figures discussed in the text are in the bibliography, and vice versa. Many names are dropped casually in the course of these fictional conversations, and it seems superfluous to amplify them. The chief exception is the work of Davydov itself. I have endeavored to cite the page references for the Davydov quotes for the benefit of the more scholarly among *Natasha*'s readers, while recognizing that this is a compromise that might fully satisfy no one. — M. L.

Buchler, J. (1951). *Toward a general theory of human judgment*. New York: Columbia University Press.

Buchler, J. (1955). *Nature and judgment*. New York: Columbia University Press.

Buchler, J. (1966). *Metaphysics of natural complexes*. New York: Columbia University Press.

Daniels, H. (1993). *Charting the agenda: Educational activity after Vygotsky*. London and New York: Routledge.

Davydov, V. V. (1988a). The basic concept of contemporary psychology. *Soviet Education, 30*(8), 25–43.

Davydov, V. V. (1988b). Problems of children's mental development. *Soviet Education, 30*(8), 44–97.

Davydov, V. V. (1988c). Learning activity in the younger school age period. *Soviet Education, 30*(9), 3–47.

Davydov, V. V. (1988d). The mental development of younger school children in the process of learning activity. *Soviet Education, 30*(9), 48–83.

Davydov, V. V. (1988e). The mental development of younger school children in the process of learning activity [continued]. *Soviet Education, 30*(10), 3–36.

Davydov, V. V. (1995). The influence of L. S. Vygotsky on education theory, research, and practice. *Educational Research, 24*(3), 12–21.

Dewey, J. (1922). *Human nature and conduct: An introduction to social psychology*. New York: The Modern Library.

Dewey, J. (1934). *Art as experience*. New York: Minton, Balch & Co.

Dewey, J. (1958). *Experience and nature* (2nd ed.). New York: Dover. (Original work published 1929)

Dewey, J., & Bentley, A. F. (1949). *Knowing and the known*. Boston: Beacon.

Gal'perin, P. Y. (1969). Stages in the development of mental acts. In M. Cole & I. Maltzman (Eds.), *A handbook of contemporary Soviet psychology* (pp. 249–273). New York: Basic Books.

Goldstein, K. (1940). *Human nature in the light of psychology*. Cambridge, MA: Harvard University Press.

Goldstein, K. (1964). *Abstract and concrete behavior*. Chicago, IL: American Psychological Association, Northwestern University.

Harris, L. (Ed.). (1991). *Children in chaos: A philosophy for children experience*. Dubuque, IA: Kendall/Hunt.

Hegel, G. W. F. (1967). *The phenomenology of mind* (J. B. Baillie, Trans.). New York: Harper & Row. (Original work published 1807)

Lipman, M. (1973). *Contemporary aesthetics*. Boston: Allyn & Bacon.

Lipman, M. (1974). *Harry Stottlemeier's discovery*. Upper Montclair, NJ: The Institute for the Advancement of Philosophy for Children, Montclair State University.

Lipman, M. (1978). *Mark*. Upper Montclair, NJ: The Institute for the Advancement of Philosophy for Children, Montclair State University.

Lipman, M. (1978). *Suki*. Upper Montclair, NJ: The Institute for the Advancement of Philosophy for Children, Montclair State University.

Lipman, M. (1981). *Pixie*. Upper Montclair, NJ: The Institute for the Advancement of Philosophy for Children, Montclair State University.

Lipman, M. (1982). *Kio and Gus*. Upper Montclair, NJ: The Institute for the Advancement of Philosophy for Children, Montclair State University.

Lipman, M. (1983). *Lisa* (2nd ed.). Upper Montclair, NJ: The Institute for the Advancement of Philosophy for Children, Montclair State University.

Lipman, M. (1987). *Elfie*. Upper Montclair, NJ: The Institute for the Advancement of Philosophy for Children, Montclair State University.

Lipman, M. (1988). *Philosophy goes to school*. Philadelphia, PA: Temple University Press.

Lipman, M. (1991). *Thinking in education*. New York: Cambridge University Press.

Lipman, M. (Ed.). (1993). *Thinking children and education*. Dubuque, IA: Kendall/Hunt.

Lipman, M., & Sharp, A. M. (Eds.). (1978). *Growing up with philosophy*. Philadelphia: Temple University Press.

Lipman, M., & Gazzard, A. (1988). *Getting our thoughts together: Elfie manual*. Upper Montclair, NJ: The Institute for the Advancement of Philosophy for Children, Montclair State University.

Lipman, M., & Sharp, A. M. (1980a). *Social inquiry: Mark manual*. Upper Montclair, NJ: The Institute for the Advancement of Philosophy for Children, Montclair State University.

Lipman, M., & Sharp, A. M. (1980b). *Writing: How and why — Suki manual*. Upper Montclair, NJ: The Institute for the Advancement of Philosophy for Children, Montclair State University.

Lipman, M., & Sharp, A. M. (1985). *Ethical inquiry: Lisa manual* (2nd ed.). Upper Montclair, NJ: The Institute for the Advancement of Philosophy for Children, Montclair State University.

Lipman, M., & Sharp, A. M. (1986). *Wondering at the world: Kio and Gus manual*. Upper Montclair, NJ: The Institute for the Advancement of Philosophy for Children, Montclair State University.

Lipman, M., Sharp, A. M., & Oscanyan, F. (1980). *Philosophy in the classroom* (2nd ed.). Philadelphia, PA: Temple University Press.

Lipman, M., Sharp, A. M., & Oscanyan, F. (1984). *Philosophical inquiry: Harry Stottlemeier's discovery manual* (rev. ed.). Upper Montclair, NJ: The Institute for the Advancement of Philosophy for Children, Montclair State University.

Matthews, G. B. (1980). *Philosophy and the young child.* Cambridge, MA: Harvard University Press.

Matthews, G. B. (1984). *Dialogues with children.* Cambridge, MA: Harvard University Press.

McDermott, J. J. (Ed.). (1973). *The philosophy of John Dewey: Vol. 1. The structure of experience.* New York: G. P. Putnam & Sons.

Mead, G. H. (1934). *Mind, self and society.* Chicago, IL: University of Chicago Press.

Moll, L. C. (Ed.). (1990). *Vygotsky and education: Instructional implications and applications of sociohistorical psychology.* Cambridge and New York: Cambridge University Press.

Neill, A. S. (1960). *Summerhill.* New York: Hart.

Orwell, G. (1949). *1984.* New York: Harcourt Brace.

Piaget, J. (1976). *The grasp of consciousness.* Cambridge, MA: Harvard University Press.

Ratner, J. (Ed.). (1939). *Intelligence in the modern world: John Dewey's philosophy.* New York: The Modern Library.

Rogoff, B. (1990). *Apprenticeship in teaching.* New York: Oxford University Press.

Sharp, A. M., & Reed, R. F. (Eds.), with Lipman, M. (1992). *Studies in philosophy for children: Harry Stottlemeier's discovery.* Philadelphia: Temple University Press.

Simmel, G. (trans. 1964). *The sociology of George Simmel.* Glencoe, IL: The Free Press.

Valéry, P. (trans. 1964). The man and the sea shell (Ralph Manheim, Trans.). In Jackson Matthews (Ed.), *The collected works of Paul Valéry* (Bollingen series XLV, Vol. 13, *Aesthetics*). Princeton, NJ: Princeton University Press.

Vygotsky, L. S. (trans. 1971). *The psychology of art.* Cambridge, MA: MIT Press.

Vygotsky, L. S. (trans. 1978). *Mind in society: The development of higher psychological processes.* (M. Cole, V. John-Steiner, S. Scribner, & E. Souberman, Eds.). Cambridge, MA: Harvard University Press.

Vygotsky, L. S. (trans. 1962). *Thought and language.* Cambridge, MA: MIT press.

Vygotsky, L. S. (trans. 1987). *The collected works of L. S. Vygotsky.* New York: Plenum.

Wertsch, J. V. (Ed.). (1985). *Culture, communication and cognition: Vygotskyan perspectives.* New York: Cambridge University Press.

Wertsch, J. V. (1985). *Vygotsky and the social formation of mind.* Cambridge, MA: Harvard University Press.

INDEX

ABOUT THE AUTHOR

Matthew Lipman is the director of the Institute for the Advancement of Philosophy for Children at Montclair State University (New Jersey) and a professor of philosophy at Montclair State University. Since taking his Ph.D. in philosophy from Columbia University in 1953, he has been awarded a doctor of letters degree from Quincy University (Illinois) and a *docteur honoris causa* degree from the University de Mons-Hainaut (Belgium). A former Fulbright scholar and Rockefeller Scholar, he was a co-winner of the 1956 Matchette Prize in Aesthetics, and the subject of a 1990 BBC documentary, *Socrates for Six-Year-Olds*. The founder of the Philosophy for Children program, he is the author of numerous books, most recently *Thinking in Education* (Cambridge University Press, 1991), and his works have been translated into 20 languages. In 1995, he was designated Distinguished University Scholar at Montclair State University.